"I DIE DAILY"

1 Corinthians 15:31
*Daily Presenting our Bodies
a Living Sacrifice*

Todd Tomasella

authorHOUSE®

AuthorHouse™
1663 Liberty Drive, Suite 200
Bloomington, IN 47403
www.authorhouse.com
Phone: 1-800-839-8640

First published by AuthorHouse 7/17/2009

ISBN: 978-1-4389-6827-8 (sc)
ISBN: 978-1-4389-7042-4 (hc)

Printed in the United States of America
Bloomington, Indiana

This book is printed on acid-free paper.

Cover Design By: April Barnett
www.corporateface.com

Other Works Available by Todd Tomasella

Raised Up (book)

Lie of the Ages: History's Fatal Falsehood (book)

Deceivers & False Prophets Among Us Vol. I (book)

LOSER (Gospel tract to win souls)

Diary of a Dead man (soul-winning Gospel tract)

JESUS: Why Did This Man Die on a Cross? (evangelistic tract)

SECRETS from Beyond the Grave (devil-chasing tract)

For the latest resources, please visit www.SafeGuardYourSoul.com

ACKNOWLEDGEMENTS

Much gratitude to the friends who helped with the production of this volume. Thanks to April Barnett for the cover design and for her wonderful husband Keith and 7 beautiful children for lending her to this project. Much gratitude to Bill Wegener for his invaluable help with many things concerning this ministry. God richly bless Melissa Robinson, Sally Matthews, and Susan Salazar for their contributions to this work.

ARE YOU AT PEACE WITH GOD?

To best understand and appreciate the contents of this volume will require personal knowledge of the One whom this author believes has inspired this writing. Friend, do you know you are at peace with God? Are you 100% sure you would go to Heaven to be with Jesus Christ if you died today? If you are 99.9% or less sure, please go to the rear of this book right now and make peace with Him. See the Making Peace with God page at the end of this book (page 203). The LORD wants to bless you with the forgiveness of all your sins and the assurance of knowing Him and knowing you are going to be with Him when you leave this earth – which could be this very day.

Take this step now and your life will be changed forever. You will be eternally grateful to the LORD and Savior Jesus Christ for His gift of eternal life, which He single-handedly purchased for us with His sinless blood.

Foreword

by Travis Bryan III

This great book focuses in on the most important message to the church today, the cross of Christ and the daily cross for all who will know and follow the LORD. There will never be revival until believers yield and die to self. In these pages, Todd Tomasella shows us the way of the cross, a way which he understands and acknowledges that he himself is daily learning.

One godly reformer referred to the Christian life as a daily baptism, or 'dying upward.' The flesh begins with birth; spirit begins with death. This applies daily, too. The daily door to the Spirit walk is our death with Christ - our daily dying to self (Rom 8:36; 12:1-2; 1 Cor. 15:31, 36; 2 Cor. 4:10-12). Daily dying is gain (we gain more of Christ). In the last days, men will be lovers of their own selves. We are to hate our old self, not love him (Jn. 12:25). In Galatians 2:20, the Greek verb is in the perfect tense: 'I have been and continue to be crucified with Christ.' The word 'planted' in Romans 6:5 is also in the perfect tense. The Valley of Achor (troubling or horror) is a door of hope (Hosea 2:14-17: Josh 7:24, 26; Isa. 65:10). To be brought low as in Psalm 116, is to die to self.

The cross is in the Spirit. It is through the Spirit that we are able to MORTIFY (crucify) the sinful deeds of the body (Rom. 8:13; Col. 3:5). Those who belong to Christ have CRUCIFIED the lusts of the flesh (Gal. 5:24).

NOTE FROM THE AUTHOR

> "For thou art great, and doest wondrous things: thou art God alone. Teach me thy way, O LORD; I will walk in thy truth: unite my heart to fear thy name. I will praise thee, O Lord my God, with all my heart: and I will glorify thy name for evermore. For great is thy mercy toward me: and thou hast delivered my soul from the lowest hell." **Psalms 86:10-13**

This writer believes there has never been a man more in need of God's all-sufficient grace than this depraved soul whom the LORD has so graciously found, regenerated, and is daily transforming for His holy, eternal purposes (Rom. 6-8; Eph.3:11). He has truly and more than the initial time **"delivered my soul from the lowest hell."** (Ps. 86:13)

> "For we ourselves also were sometimes foolish, disobedient, deceived, serving divers lusts and pleasures, living in malice and envy, hateful, *and* hating one another. But after that the kindness and love of God our Saviour toward man appeared, Not by works of righteousness which we have done, but according to his mercy he saved us, by the washing of regeneration, and renewing of the Holy Ghost; Which he shed on us abundantly through Jesus Christ our Saviour; That being justified by

his grace, we should be made heirs according to the hope of eternal life." Titus 3:3-7

All comments concerning this book are welcomed. If anyone can clearly and through the preponderance of Holy Scripture, demonstrate that anything in this book is not aligned with the mind of Christ as revealed in the full-counsel of His Word, please bring that valid concern to my attention so that correction can be made immediately.

todd@SafeGuardYourSoul.com

This writer has been himself deluded due to lack of knowledge, and wishes to assist others in biblically and spiritually discerning, that they might be spared deception and derailment and fully glorify the LORD who bought them with His precious blood.

> **"Whom having not seen, ye love; in whom, though now ye see *him* not, yet believing, ye rejoice with joy unspeakable and full of glory: Receiving the end of your faith, *even* the salvation of *your* souls." 1 Peter 1:8-9**

His watchmen are to hear and warn.

> **"So thou, O son of man, I have set thee a watchman unto the house of Israel; therefore thou shalt hear the word at my mouth, and warn them from me... Therefore, thou son of man, say unto the children of thy people, The righteousness of the righteous shall not deliver him in the day of his transgression: as for the wickedness of the wicked, he shall not fall thereby in the day that he turneth from his wickedness; neither shall the righteous be able to live for his *righteousness* in the day that he sinneth. When I shall say to the righteous, *that* he shall surely live; if he trust to his own righteousness, and**

commit iniquity, all his righteousnesses shall not be remembered; but for his iniquity that he hath committed, he shall die for it." Ezekiel 33:7, 12-13

The LORD told His watchman to "**hear the word at my mouth, and warn them from me.**" Like the prophet Ezekiel, the body of Christ is to **"hear"** the Word of God and **"warn"** others of false doctrines which war against revealed truth, corrupting the image and will of the living God in the hearts of men, namely His own people. A **"watchman"** or overseer in the body of Christ is to **"earnestly contend for the faith which was once delivered unto the saints,"** declaring, defending and guarding the divine oracles, and speaking according to them alone (Isa. 8:20; 2 Tim. 4:2-5; 1 Pet. 4:11; Jude 3-4).

The deep concern of this writer and an army of God-fearing men and women, is that without biblical authority, multitudes are being led to believe in a cross-less "Christianity" that is not the original Gospel delivered to us by Christ and His holy apostles. Divine truth protects, and it is our prayer that this volume will be an educational tool for individuals and groups, springboarding each reader into a life of allegiance to Jesus Christ first and foremost. It is also our desire and prayer that each reader would become a doer of divine truth and follow His call to die to self – to be buried deep in the death and burial of Christ – that Jesus Christ might reign supreme in each individual life and among all His saints for whom He shall soon return.

For the latest resources, please visit www. SafeGuardYourSoul.com

Table of Contents

The Reason for this Volume

To illustrate the need for such Bible based teaching, let's take a look at this email received leading up to the publication of this volume. We assume that this email likely came from a sincere yet deceived person who is seeking the truth. We were glad to receive it and prayerfully speak into this person's life. God bless them richly in Jesus Christ.

EMAIL RESPONSE TO THIS BOOK TITLE, *I Die Daily*:

> "I wouldn't buy a book that says 'I die daily.' Solutions are needed, not dying. Why buy a book you think is about dying daily and not healing ..."

Our response to this email went something like this:

> Hi, and thank you for taking time to comment. In answer to your comment, I would respond this way: According to Christ and His apostles, dying IS the solution, the only solution - that Christ might reign in our bodies and not us - "I am crucified with Christ: nevertheless I live; yet not I, but Christ liveth in me: and the life which I now live in the flesh I live by the faith of the Son of God, who loved me, and gave himself for me." (Galatians 2:20) "He must increase, but I must decrease." (Jn. 3:30) The deceiver (false prophet 'Christian' author) would entice the buyers - make merchandise of them - by alluring them

through the lust of the flesh to buy his book, which is purposely entitled to attract those looking to salvage what God said must die - the flesh, the sinful nature, the self-will, self-effort, self-aggrandizement, self-esteem, etc. This is why you have the titles you have today – "Best Life Now," and other reinventing yourself type titles. All these deceivers who are set forth by Satan to lead millions astray - and that is what is happening – their books sell by the millions. The titles and messages are based on the diabolical premise of salvaging the sinful or carnal part of us, which Christ and His apostles commanded us to crucify. Paul said that there was "NO good thing" in him except Jesus Christ (Rom. 7:18).

The resurrection life of Christ is only given to those who choose to obey Him by crucifying the deeds of the body and fellowshipping with Him in the death of His/their personal will (Lk. 22:42; Rom. 6; 2 Cor. 4:10-11; Phil. 3:10; etc.).

And yes, laying down your life is what dying daily is - "And he said to them all, If any man will come after me, let him DENY HIMSELF, and take up his cross (implement of death) daily, and follow me. For whosoever will save (love) his life shall lose it: but whosoever will lose his life for my sake, the same shall save it." (Luke 9:23-24)

The "healing" is the resurrection, but it cannot come and will not come until the individual chooses to daily and experientially die and be buried with Christ.

God's blessings to you in Jesus Christ.

Such a conversation underscores the need for this essential biblical topic to be studied and understood by all who will follow Christ (Hos. 4:6; Matt. 22:29).

On Literary Style......

This writer is privileged to have been found and saved by Christ, and is learning daily to become His servant. No desire exists of becoming famous, but rather to obey Christ's command to feed His precious sheep (Jn. 21:15-17; 1 Pet. 5:1-6). In keeping with this governing truth, there will be times of restating Bible verses in order to teach by repetition and association. This volume is intentionally Scripture-rich in accordance with Ezekiel 3:4, 2 Timothy 4:2, and 1 Peter 4:11. The LORD's words are divinely filled with wealth. Whether it is the very first or 70th time we have looked at the same word, verse, or passage, new light is always given to those who humbly and diligently **"search the scriptures."** (Jn. 5:39; Acts 17:11)

There are times when the same Bible text or verse applies and is appropriate to show again. **"Study"** requires focus on a verse, word, or Bible topic, and repetition is key in learning (2 Tim. 2:15). Jesus memorized Scripture, and so should every one of His followers (Prov. 4:4; Lk. 4:4, 8, 10, 17-21). This rescued soul shall never forget how the LORD found and saved him, and early on blessed his life with a pastor faithful to God's eternal Truth. The first pastor He directed me to learn under was a man whose conscience was captive to God's holy Truth, who would often have a theme Bible verse in his messages, which he would repeat several times while delivering that living Word. On many an occasion, one would have that inspired verse memorized before leaving that meeting. God be praised! The wisdom of Heaven says: **"He taught me also, and said unto me, Let thine heart retain my words: keep my commandments, and live."** (Prov. 4:4)

"This book of the law shall not depart out of thy mouth; but thou shalt meditate therein day and night, that thou mayest observe to do according to all that is written therein: for then thou shalt make thy way prosperous, and then thou shalt have good success." Joshua 1:8

Chapter One

"The Cross"

"But God forbid that I should glory, save in the cross of our Lord Jesus Christ, by whom the world is crucified unto me, and I unto the world." Galatians 6:14

"The cross" is all about relationship. **"The blood of His cross"** purchased us back to God from sin (Acts 20:28; Col. 1:20). *Paul here says in essence that His love for the Savior, who bled for his sins, warranted his full allegiance to Him and crucifixion with Him. Nothing was more important to this servant apostle than knowing God and remaining in Him* (1 Cor. 9:27; Phil. 3:7-10). All else was counted as **"dung"** compared to the surpassing importance of his relationship with Jesus Christ. This is the **"mark"** he pressed toward with all of his being (Phil. 3:7-14). Paul knew the eternal danger of not keeping under the sins of his body and in the end becoming a **"castaway."** (1 Cor. 9:27) He was fully aware of the 5 specific sins that kept God's own people out of their promised land, and would keep him out of the promised land of Heaven if he allowed his sinful nature, which was at **"enmity against God,"** to rule in his life, bringing defilement in the eyes of a holy God (Mk. 7:20-23; Rom. 8:7; 1 Cor. 9:27-10:12; Heb.

1

12:14-16). God's will is to bring people **"out from"** spiritual death and **"in"** the place of His life, that He might preserve them alive (with His life – Deut. 6:23-24; Rom. 8:1-13).

The purpose and point of **"the cross"** is not that God is trying to deprive anyone of something valuable, but rather that He seeks relationship with that person – **"for our good always."** (Deut. 6:23-24) It is by the blood of Christ's cross that we are saved, and **"through faith"** in Him that we are **"kept."** (1 Pet. 1:5) Those in Him must **"endure to the end."** (Matt. 10:22; 24:13)

It is **"the goodness of God leadeth thee to repentance."** (Rom. 2:4) From the beginning, He made us for relationship with Him (Exod. 25:8). This is why Jesus came to the earth - **"And this is life eternal (the reason for it), <u>that they might know thee the only true God, and Jesus Christ</u>, whom thou hast sent."** (Jn. 17:3)

Since the LORD is holy, and the self-life or nature is sinful and at enmity with Him, it must be put to death because He who is **"holy, holy, holy"** will not commune with a sinful vessel (Isa. 6:3; 59:2; 2 Cor. 6:14-7:1; 1 Jn. 1:3-9; Rev. 4:8). Sin breaks that fellowship (Rom. 6:23). Like it or not, **"the wages of sin is"** still spiritual **"death"** and always will be, due to God's eternal and unchangeable nature of holiness. The cross of Christ is the answer.

Holiness or pureness of heart and thought is of supreme importance in the eyes of the Almighty. His eyes are upon our hearts and the thoughts that we are dwelling upon (1 Sam. 16:7; Ps. 51:10; 139:23-24; Prov. 15:3; Matt. 5:8; Acts 15:9). The cross, which must be daily applied to the inner life by the disciple, is the implement of death to the sinfully self-loving, self-driven, self-willed, and self-consumed life. The fervent worship of Jesus, which always leads one to the application of the cross, brings the glorious liberty that only Christ can grant – to be fully filled, led, and made free by the Holy Ghost of God.

One manifests his love in relationship with God when he chooses to obey Him in denying the sinful deeds of the sinful nature, in order that he might commune with and serve the Father and Savior, who died on the cross to reconcile him to the One who is **"holy, holy, holy."** (Isa. 6:3; 1 Jn. 1:3-10; Rev. 4:8) Otherwise, sin will prevent his relationship with the LORD. Sin must be confessed to be cleansed (1 Jn. 1:9). Saving faith will always drive one to obey Christ, which includes the premium He places on His people being **"pure in heart."** (Matt. 5:8; 1 Jn. 2:3-5; James 1:22) Christ told us that only the **"pure in heart"** will be **"blessed."** (Matt. 5:8) If one who has been saved goes back and ceases to obey Christ, it's because he no longer loves Christ supremely, nor does he now possess saving faith (1 Tim. 5:12; 2 Tim. 4:10; James 2; 2 Pet. 2:20-21).

If a person does not want more of Jesus, he is not a part of the remnant of Christ's elect (Rev. 17:14). If a person is always looking to circumvent the **"daily"** cross, and looking for doctrinal ways to justify not giving over his whole will and being to Christ, he is willingly lost (Rom. 12:1). Those who are truly His **"depart from iniquity,"** as they daily **"present"** their **"bodies a living sacrifice, holy and acceptable unto God."** (Rom. 12:1; 2 Tim. 2:19)

If one will guard his heart and be preserved to the end in his relationship with Christ, he must beware of the numerous cross-less and Calvinistic wolves who occupy positions of leadership and influence in the modern church world. Millions have already been deceived and will be shocked on Judgment Day (Matt. 7:15-23; Lk. 13:27-28).

The LORD bless you richly today, and fill you with His Holy Ghost afresh to subdue your own self-life, that Jesus' life might be manifested in your life (2 Cor. 4:10-12). God is able as we do things His way. His grace is fully sufficient for us (Rom. 6:14; 1 Cor. 15:10; 2 Cor. 12:9-10).

In God's economy, holiness in His people is a must, and it's the blood of Christ that enables the recipient and possessor of His salvation to experience overcoming victory through the cross (Rom. 6; Heb. 12:14; 1 Pet. 1:15-16; Rev. 21:8, 27). His enabling grace was made possible though Christ's redemption, and there is therefore no excuse for living in sin (Rom. 6). There can be no variance from such biblical truth in true Christian preaching. Sin separates and hell awaits all who die in sin – no matter what their previous relationship with God may have been (Rev. 21:8, 27; 22:11, 15). Relationship with Christ, personal holiness, the cross, overcoming sin, and repentance, go hand in hand; and today, none of these essentials can be found prevalent in the mouths of most so-called "Christian" pastors, writers, and leaders (Isa. 9:16; 1 Cor. 1:18; Phil. 3:18-19). By **"the blood of his cross,"** Christ made us holy in our *position* with God, and He commands each of us to take up our own cross and count ourselves crucified with Him in our daily lives, that His holiness might be manifest *experientially* in our lives (Rom. 6; 2 Cor. 4:10-11; Gal. 2:20).

David Kupelian, vice president and managing editor of *WorldNetDaily.com*, writes:

> **"'I die daily'**
>
> In ages past, Christians dwelt a lot more on the concept of taking up the 'cross' than they do these days. Today, the phrase 'it's my cross to bear' is usually a somewhat self-congratulatory reference to the fact that we have to put up with a vexing medical condition, or a child in trouble with the law, or perhaps an overbearing, live-in mother-in-law.

Admonitions from the pulpit may not shed much more light. Oh sure, a well-intentioned minister will reverently read one of the scriptures cited above on 'taking up the cross,' and he might even briefly plug the ideal of self-denial. But too often this amounts to a polite nod to a notion that seems both archaic and almost irrelevant, or at least unattainable, and the pastor just moves on to more pleasant topics – like how grateful we are that we're saved by Christ's death and resurrection.

It wasn't always so. Throughout past centuries, Christian philosophers and mystics dwelt at length on the crucial, life-and-death need for repentance, resignation, 'mortification,' the 'crucifixion' of sin in man, and the 'death of the carnal man' or of 'the creaturely self' and so on.

The Apostle Paul said it most powerfully and succinctly when he wrote: 'I die daily.'"

If they are not crucified on the cross we are instructed to **"take up,"** the deeds of the body will cause one to displease the LORD by the manifestation of the soul-damning **"works of the flesh."** (Gal. 5:19-21)

The Two Cross Deaths

There are two kinds of dying seen in the Scriptures – *positional* and *experiential*.

Positional death speaks of our oneness with the death Christ experienced when He died on the cross, when he did **"taste death for every man."** (Heb. 2:9) *Positionally* we are dead and buried with Him (Rom. 6:3-4).

Experiential death of the inner self-life = the willing crucifixion of the personal will out of a far surpassing love for and desire to see Christ reign supreme. *When we love*

Him more than ourselves, we will die so He can live. Life can only spring out of death (Jn. 12:24). The problem is that most people who claim to be Christians love themselves more than Christ (2 Tim. 3:1-7). They have freely chosen to resist loving the LORD with all of their hearts, souls, minds, and strength (Matt. 22:37-40).

The Positional Cross

The word **"baptized"** is used in more than one way in the Bible. It is used to express both a literal and a figurative immersion. Immersion simply means *being placed all the way into*. In Romans 6, speaking figuratively of our baptism into Christ (not water), the apostle writes:

> **"Know ye not, that so many of us as were baptized into Jesus Christ were baptized into his death? Therefore <u>we are buried with him by baptism into death</u>: that like as Christ was raised up from the dead by the glory of the Father, even so we also should walk in newness of life." Romans 6:3-4**

We have been immersed (baptized) completely into Christ figuratively - **"we are buried with him by baptism into death."**

Our justification and sanctification are wrapped up in being buried with Christ. We are then risen with Him and enabled to **"walk in newness of life."** Our *position* – buried with and in Christ – enables the literally manifested life of Christ to be *experienced* in our daily lives.

We are united with Christ in His death, burial, and resurrection. The phrase **"in Christ,"** seen throughout New Testament Scripture, is short for our immersion into Him – His death, burial, and resurrection and our own death, burial, and resurrection with Him. Jesus died and was raised up once, and we died and are raised up with Him in type/proxy.

> **"Even when we were dead in sins, hath quickened us (made us alive) together with Christ, (by grace ye are saved;) And hath raised us up together, and made us sit together in heavenly places in Christ Jesus: That in the ages to come he might shew the exceeding riches of his grace in his kindness toward us through Christ Jesus." Ephesians 2:5-7**

THE LORD has **"raised up"** those He has found and saved out of their sinful state and into His eternal kingdom. They are **"raised up"** to **"sit together"** with Him – **"in heavenly places in Christ Jesus."** This He did for His eternal purposes. He **"made us sit together in heavenly places in Christ Jesus,"** so this is our *positional* standing with Him; yet His desire is that such a *positional* place become an *experiential* reality in our **"daily"** lives, as we **"follow"** Him. And how does such a translation happen? This manifested **"newness of life"** occurs as we lay down our self-will in full surrender to His Majesty, crying out **"Father, into thy hands I commend my spirit."** (Lk. 23:46) Victorious living in this **"newness of life"** happens when we follow His instructions to **"deny"** ourselves and **"take up"** the cross, and let His will and life reign in our mortal bodies in place of our own. This *positional* seating in Christ and with God in heavenly places becomes a reality in our daily *experience* as we sentence our lives to death, being rooted in Christ, as we **"take root downward."** (Isa 37:31) He then raises us upward in **"newness of life"** – with His life to bear fruit to His pleasing.

Our *positional* place with Him means that we died with Him, and we are seated in heavenly places in Christ. Yet, we are still on earth and subject to temptations. This is why the *experiential* cross is so important.

7

The Experiential Cross

> "For if we have been planted together in the likeness of his death, we shall be also in the likeness of his resurrection: Knowing this, that our old man is crucified with him, that the body of sin might be destroyed, that henceforth we should not serve sin. For he that is dead is freed from sin." Romans 6:5-6

The believer, who is buried with Christ and risen in **"newness of life,"** is told that he **"should not serve sin."** Serving sin or the Savior is always going to be a choice as long as we are on the earth.

> "For sin shall not have dominion over you: for ye are not under the law, but under grace." Romans 6:14

In studying the subject of dying daily and Paul's words in 1 Corinthians 15:31, **"I die daily,"** I have read a few commentaries which seemed to only acknowledge the *positional* death of the believer. This is because the misguided Calvinist wants no part of anything that might cost him the suffering of death to his own will. He wants to believe that God did it all, and subsequently ignores the commandments of the very same God for him to personally experience dying to self and self-will. The Calvinist is a moral coward who wants the crown without the cross, so he objects to and flees any notion of personal responsibility. In the face of a mountain of Scriptural commands and conditional blessings, he insists that there are no requirements placed upon him. If that were so, why then the many commandments of Christ and His holy apostles? The diabolical dynamic of Calvinism is to escape and deny by any means possible, any teaching that calls for a personal cost. In contrast, the Bible teaches us that to lose is to gain (Matt. 10:38-39; Jn. 12:24-26; Phil. 1:21). The spiritual coward wants to hide away in his false security zone, where he is protected from all that would cause him to suffer – the circumcising sword of the Word, persecutions, tribulations, dying to sin and self, purgings, and the chastening of the LORD. This is why this theology always migrates to the line of least resistance to the flesh – no baptism in the Holy Spirit or lordship of Christ, due to the myth of 'once saved always saved,' and a pre-tribulation rapture. (Actually, although he holds no strong position on the exact timing of Christ's return, this writer believes that there is the possibility of a pre-tribulation rapture. In the previous statement, I was just making a point.)

Some may despise the idea that people teach the Scripture **"I die daily"** as something that needs to be done by the individual recipient of salvation. The Calvinistically infected mindset believes that everything that needs to be done has already been done, and that man has no choice or accountability in the matter of participation. It's true that Christ initiated and earned our salvation, and that without Him we are hopeless. It is also just as true that this same Jesus instructed those who would follow Him to be **"daily"** crucified with Him, by denying themselves and taking up their crosses. Romans 6 says, **"Our old man is crucified with him"** (v 6), and yet it also says:

- **"What shall we say then? Shall we continue in sin, that grace may abound?"** (v 1) – The question **"Shall we"** denotes volition, option, and choice.

- **"For if we have been planted together in the likeness of his death, we shall be also in the likeness of his resurrection."** (v 5) – The **"if"** here speaks of volition, option, and choice.

- **"Reckon ye also yourselves to be dead indeed unto sin, but alive unto God through Jesus Christ our Lord."** (v 11)

9

- "Let not sin therefore reign in your mortal body, that ye should obey it in the lusts thereof." (v 12)

- "Neither yield ye your members as instruments of unrighteousness unto sin: but yield yourselves unto God, as those that are alive from the dead, and your members as instruments of righteousness unto God." (v 13)

- "Know ye not, that to whom ye yield yourselves servants to obey, his servants ye are to whom ye obey; whether of sin unto death, or of obedience unto righteousness?" (v 16)

The honest student of the Bible, the one that refuses to allow himself to be infected with any predisposed notion, will see this.

The work of Christ to *position* us in heavenly places is a settled fact and truth (Eph. 2:6). As we are discovering from Holy Writ, the *experiential* cross of the individual must be taken up and died upon. Paul the apostle of Christ said, **"I KEEP under my body."** (1 Cor. 9:27) The denial of the self-life and following Jesus is only accomplished by the enabling grace and Holy Spirit of the LORD, who is perfecting that which concerns us as He continues His good work in us – we who have been apprehended by Him for His purpose and glory (Ps. 138:8; Phil. 1:6; 2:12-13). This occurs as we **"work out"** our **"salvation with fear and trembling."** (Phil. 2:12-13) It is "**through the Spirit**" that we are blessed and empowered to **"mortify the deeds of the body."** (Rom. 8:13)

There are those who know only the *positional* application of the cross, where we **"are dead"** and buried with Christ, and raised up by the faith of the operation of God, and seated together in heavenly places in Christ (Rom. 6:3-4; Eph. 2:6; Col. 3:3). In spite of understanding that we are dead, buried, and raised up with Christ, men misunderstand or do not know about the doctrine of the daily cross – the keeping under or subduing of the sinful nature on a daily basis. The essential nature of such a biblical and vital truth is tragically seldom, if ever, spoken about in most "ministry" that transpires in the modern church world.

Love is a daily test.

Love is a daily choice.

That person who has a mere **"form of godliness"** and yet denies the power of Christ to reign in his life, will never experience the fellowship of His sufferings and the blessed **"fruit"** He desires to bring forth **"upward"** to His glory (Isa. 37:31; Rom. 8:11; 2 Tim. 3:5). Many seek to render rote adherence to the command of Christ while lacking the *positional* revelation of the death, burial, and resurrection of the Gospel. In contrast, the true disciple of Christ is that one who is driven by the greater desire and love that possesses his heart for Christ. His love for Jesus far surpasses his love for self and the pleasures of this world.

Throughout Holy Scripture, we are afforded the blessing of witnessing the joyful delight many had for the LORD. Here is a sampling:

> **"Whom have I in heaven but thee? and there is none upon earth that I desire beside thee." Psalms 73:25**

> **"That I may know him, and the power of his resurrection, and the fellowship of his sufferings, being made conformable unto his death ... Brethren, I count not myself to have apprehended: but this one thing I do, forgetting those things which are behind, and reaching forth unto those things which are before, I press toward the mark**

for the prize of the high calling of God in Christ Jesus." Philippians 3:10, 13-14

"One thing have I desired of the LORD, that will I seek after; that I may dwell in the house of the LORD all the days of my life, to behold the beauty of the LORD, and to enquire in his temple." Psalms 27:4

The **"one thing"** that most deeply and profoundly moved these men and women was knowing Him more and more, seeking His face in earnest as they experienced Him daily.

"Behold, what manner of love the Father hath bestowed upon us, that we should be called the sons of God: therefore the world knoweth us not, because it knew him not." 1 John 3:1

The love we are blessed to possess of Him, and the cross, go hand in hand. Because of His love in us, and our own decision to reciprocate that love, we make a daily choice to experience the cross. The daily cross is the application of death applied into our life and will, in order that Christ's will and life might be in control and reign in our mortal bodies (2 Cor. 4:10-12).

God made man with a choice (Deut. 30:19; Josh. 24:15; Gal. 6:7-9). Firstly, it makes no sense at all biblically speaking, to say that the person and volitional will of the individual believer plays no part in his decisions. That is a diabolical and Calvinistic heresy that has no biblical ground beneath it. Those in denial of the cross Jesus commanded us to **"daily"** take up, simply do not wish to deny self and sin as Christ commanded. Many of them have placed the teachings of mere men – who were heretics – above God's Word. Instead of setting aside the **"doctrines of men"** for Christ's teachings, they set the teachings of the Son of God aside for the teachings of mere men (like John Calvin). Like the Pharisees of Christ's day, these men love their traditions more than the LORD and His Word (Mk. 7:6-9). Every generation in history has its pseudo-theologians, who cast away the Word of God for their own traditions of mere men. Every day also has a remnant, which says, **"Let God be true and every man a liar."** (Rom. 3:4)

Letting **"God be true"** in our personal lives includes silencing the call of the sinful nature, Satan, and the voices of the myriad of cross-denying wolves, who come in Christ's name yet do not preach His original Gospel.

> **"And he said to them all, If any man will come after me, let him deny himself, and take up his cross daily, and follow me." Luke 9:23**

Throughout His teachings, the Son of God taught us that following Him was a **"daily"** *experience* and not a one-time event. He made it abundantly clear that this **"daily"** *experience* of His life was only possible in conjunction with the disciple's self-denial, and his choosing to prefer the Savior above himself (Matt. 16:24-26; Lk. 9:23-24; Jn. 12:23-26).

> "Many admit the *positional* death (at initial salvation), but there is also a present salvation (progressive sanctification or transformation) that is *experiential*, the daily death, burial and resurrection. The Leviticus 1 burnt offering occurred daily. The first thing the invader always did at the Temple was to do away with the daily sacrifice. This will also be 1st order of business for the antichrist, and for those who possess the spirit of antichrist today." Travis Bryan III

Christ told us that if we would follow Him, we must **"daily"** take up the cross and follow (Lk. 9:23-24). As Travis Bryan III has pointed out here, the daily sacrifice is attacked by the invader and enemy of our souls, and this is seen in the absence of such preaching in that which calls itself the church today. The Bible tells us that **"Satan"** has his **"ministers,"** and these men are **"deceitful workers"** who have infiltrated the modern church and so-called higher learning institutions (seminaries, etc.). See 2 Cor. 11:12-15. These **"false apostles,"** who are imposters, have hi-jacked the pulpits and publishing houses of this last hour with a message that is void of the cross and is sending many to eternal darkness (2 Pet. 2:1-3). They can be identified as the **"enemies of the cross of Christ,"** who do not take up their own crosses daily, and therefore do not preach the cross as a daily implement of death to self and self-denial (2 Cor. 11:12-15; Phil. 3:18-19). Instead, they **"mind earthly things,"** even using Scripture to justify their misplaced affections (Phil. 3:18-19).

The **"adversary, the devil,"** can **"devour"** us by drawing and seducing us out from our daily and *experiential* death and burial with Christ, where we are **"hid with Christ in God."** (Col. 3:3) When the enemy is able to draw one out into the open, he is then vulnerable as a deer that comes out of the forest and is no longer hidden and protected by the camouflage of the trees. When a deer is out in the open and in a prairie clearing, he is then prey for predators. The lions can then see and smell him, and will seek to devour him.

Taking up the daily cross and *experiencing* knowing Him in **"the fellowship of his sufferings"** demonstrates our agreement with God that we are utterly depraved in our Adamic nature, and wholly in need of His righteousness and life to reign in our **"mortal"** bodies (Rom. 6; 2 Cor. 4:10-11; Phil. 3:10).

In this following passage, watch for the daily *experiential* cross to be practiced by every true disciple of Jesus:

14

> **"Always (daily) bearing about in the body the dying of the Lord Jesus, <u>that</u> the life also of Jesus might be made manifest (a reality) in our body. For we which live are alway (daily) delivered unto death for Jesus' sake, <u>that</u> the life also of Jesus might be made manifest in our mortal flesh." 2 Corinthians 4:10-11**

As we related earlier in this chapter, the removal of the **"daily"** cross is the work of our **"adversary."** The same vulnerability (removal of the daily cross) exists today wherever the redeemed saint allows for the **"daily"** sacrifice to be stolen from his life. The daily presenting of ourselves to Him as **"a living sacrifice"** is our **"reasonable service"** in light of what He has done for us (Rom. 12:1).

Because He loves us as His own, Christ instructs those He saves to **"daily"** deny themselves and take up their crosses to follow Him (Lk. 9:23-24). It is only in being **"dead"** to sin and self that our lives **"are hid with Christ in God."**

> **"For ye are dead, and your life is hid with Christ in God." Colossians 3:3**

"Precious Things" Stolen

> **<u>"There is a conspiracy of her prophets (leaders) in the midst thereof,</u> like a roaring lion ravening the prey; they have devoured souls; they have taken the treasure and precious things; they have made her many widows in the midst thereof." Ezekiel 22:25**

Ezekiel the prophet of God is writing here concerning the leaders of the very nation of Israel. This **"conspiracy"** he speaks of is a *reality* and *not a theory*. We have the divine word on it here. The Bible tells us definitively here that **"There is a conspiracy of her prophets"** or leaders who claim to be representing the LORD. We are also informed

15

here that these beguilers **"have taken the treasure and precious things."** They have stolen away those things which are most important for believers to be aware of, believe, dwell upon, and do.

The enemy invader is now empowering his agents in the pulpits and those who hold the pens of modern publishing. This is seen in the deafening silence of the modern messages we hear. There is a gross lack of hearing the essential truths of Holy Writ spoken or written by men who have positions of influence. In fact, in fulfillment of last days prophecy, hordes of self-serving people (who claim to be Christians) are heaping these smooth and deceitful messages, and the messengers who give them, to themselves. Their un-crucified sinful nature seeks out ear-tickling messages that feed their sinful nature instead of beckoning them to crucify it (Rom. 6; 12:1).

In his messages, the beguiling leader feeds the sinful nature, while the leader who is a true servant of Christ calls for the denial of and death of it (Rom. 16:17-18; Phil. 3:1-3; 18-21; 2 Pet. 2:1-3).

Many who love the truth, and therefore deeply desire more of Christ, are coming out of the cross-less and apostate modern church system. Like Paul, their deep desire is **"to know him, and the power of his resurrection, and the fellowship of his sufferings, being made conformable unto his death."** (Phil. 3:10) They have seen the folly and the **"famine in the land, not a famine of bread, nor a thirst for water, <u>but of hearing the words of the LORD</u>."** (Amos 8:11)

Where We Stand

In a passage often referred to as defining the true Gospel, the apostle Paul reveals that this **"gospel"** is that **"wherein ye stand."**

"Moreover, brethren, <u>I declare unto you the gospel</u> which I preached unto you, which also ye have received, and <u>wherein ye stand</u>." 1 Corinthians 15:1-4

As those found and regenerated by Him who first loved us, we **"stand"** in the Gospel of Christ – both *positionally* and *experientially*. In fact, the very next words speak to the essential responsibility of personal participation of the individual recipient of His **"so great salvation."** (Heb. 2:3)

"By which also ye are saved, IF ye keep in memory what I preached unto you, unless ye have believed in vain." 1 Corinthians 15:2

The **"if"** here clearly denotes condition. Our salvation is contingent upon **"if"** we **"keep in memory"** the original **"gospel"** the apostle Paul preached, **"unless ye have believed in vain."** Our initial salvation becomes ineffectual if we do not **"continue"** in Christ or **"endure to the end."** (Matt. 10:22; Col. 1:23; Heb. 3:6, 12-15; 10:26-39; 2 Pet. 2:20-21)

Daily *experiencing* death to self and the raised up life of Christ, is essential to keeping in memory the work of Christ, the coming King.

See if you can identify both the *positional* and the *experiential* standing of the believer in this Colossians 3 passage:

"If ye then be risen with Christ, seek those things which are above, where Christ sitteth on the right hand of God. Set your affection on things above, not on things on the earth. For ye are dead, and your life is hid with Christ in God." Colossians 3:1-3

He has accomplished salvation for us and we are thereby **"risen with Christ,"** *positionally*. In light of this, *we* should then follow suit in seeking **"those things which are above,**

17

where Christ sitteth on the right hand of God." This includes setting our **"affection(s) on things above, not on things on the earth."** *Positionally,* we are to count ourselves **"dead,"** and consider that our lives are **"hid with Christ in God."**

Some erroneously teach that the believer's *positional* place with Christ is irreversible, but the Bible tells us differently in a myriad of places. Only when we keep our place or position **"with Christ"** are we **"hid with Christ in God."** Otherwise we are *not* hidden away from the wrath of God and the enemy. Such a place of being **"hid with Christ in God"** is conditional upon the recipient of His salvation remaining in Him. One's place with God is reversible if one does not **"abide"** or remain **"in Christ."** Jesus told us that **"If a man abide (remain) not in me, he is cast forth as a branch, and is withered; and men gather them, and cast them into the fire, and they are burned."** (Jn. 15:6) Our LORD also told us that there are those **"which for a while believe, and in time of temptation <u>fall away</u>."** (Lk. 8:13) It should be more than obvious that someone could not possibly **"fall away"** from something he has not previously possessed. Also, the basic fact that Jesus invented the term **"fall away"** plainly reveals that such is possible.

That *positional* standing He purchased for us is ours only as we remain **"with Christ,"** and **"if"** a redeemed person chooses to cease following Christ, he is no longer **"in Christ"** or **"with Christ,"** and is therefore no longer the recipient of any of His blessings. The Father told us on several occasions that it is only in His only begotten Son that He is **"well pleased,"** so anyone presently outside of Him is not pleasing to God (Matt. 3:17).

The sacrifice of Christ is a fixed reality. He is invariable and unchanging (Mal. 3:6; Jn. 19:30; James 1:17). But the experiencing of the cross of Christ in the daily life of the recipient of His salvation is volitional. One must count all else **"dung"** compared to knowing Christ, and in order to **"know him,"** one must be willing to experience **"the fellowship of his sufferings, being made conformable unto his death."** (Phil. 3:7-10).

All of Holy Scripture testifies to the truth that God's blessings to individuals are conditional (Deut. 11:26-28; 28:1-67; 30:19-20). The fulfillment of His promises and blessings are contingent upon the obedience of the individual (Gal. 6:7-9; Heb. 6:11-12). The recipient of His free gift of eternal life must by faith **"abide"** or remain in Him, or he will be **"cut off."** (Ezek. 33:12-13; Matt. 10:22; Lk. 8:13; Rom. 11:19-22; 1 Cor. 15:2; Col. 1:23; Heb. 3:6, 12-15; 10:26-39; 2 Jn. 9; Rev. 2-3) This important subject is covered extensively in the book titled *Lie of the Ages,* which can be ordered at www. SafeGuardYourSoul.com.

"Many of His Disciples Went Back"

In the record of John 6, we read of **"disciples"** who continued not with Christ after He taught them. They chose not to partake in His death and life. They did not want to suffer for His sake, and therefore **"many of his disciples went back, and walked no more with him."**

> **"From that time <u>many of his disciples went back, and walked no more with him</u>." John 6:66**

These people forfeited their place with Christ and all the associated benefits, both here and eternally (Ezek. 33:12-13). Suffering is part of following Christ, and those who **"draw back,"** not esteeming Christ and being unwilling to suffer for His sake, will lose out (Rom. 8:17; Phil. 1:29; Heb. 10:38-39; 1 Pet. 4:1-14; Rev. 2-3).

According to God's Word, those who refuse to follow up in their daily lives with *experiential* living with Christ, partaking of His blessed sufferings and the associated benefits, will lose out on their *positional* place they once had with Him (2 Pet. 2:20-21). Those who after being bought by His blood, **"deny him,"** will also be denied by Him for having **"trodden under foot the Son of God."** (2 Tim. 2:12; Heb. 10:29)

One will not experience His resurrection life if he refuses to experience a dying with Him – to self, sin, Satan, and this world.

Many today are seeking to gain, but they are trying to go around the cross. These people do not yet realize that it's only in dying to self that God's **"gain"** will come to them. It's only in dying that they can live by the resurrecting power of God in Christ, who is **"the resurrection and the life."** (Jn. 11:25) He promised to raise up by the power of His Holy Spirit those that be bowed down in death to self and sin (Ps. 145:15; Rom. 8:11). The LORD promises to raise upward in fruitfulness those that **"take root downward."** (Isa. 37:31)

The cross is the place of safety – being in the center of God's will. We are safe on the cross, buried, sunk down, and hidden in Christ while being **"raised up"** by His power and to His glory (Rom. 6:3-4; 8:11; Col. 2:11-12; 3:3). Beware of the wiles of Satan, who seeks to lure us off the cross where we are **"hid with Christ in God."** (Col. 3:3) The enemy's design is to keep you ignorant of the necessity of the cross – to keep you from experiencing Christ's resurrection power. When you do choose to learn of Christ to get on the cross, the enemy's scheme will be to get you to come down from that cross – to keep you from dying that Christ's life might reign in you and over the enemy (Lk. 10:18). Is this not what he did to our LORD? (Matt. 27:42)

The only way to have upward mobility – divine resurrection power – is to plant yourself deep into the death of Christ. The further down one descends, the more powerful the raising up will be (2 Cor. 4:10-12).

Jesus told us that we must lose our lives to gain His life and eternal life.

> **"Verily, verily, I say unto you, <u>Except</u> a corn of wheat fall into the ground and die, it abideth alone: but if it die, it bringeth forth much fruit. He that loveth his life shall lose it; and he that hateth his life in this world shall keep it unto life eternal."**
> **John 12:24-25**

PRAYER: *Father, not my will but Thine be done. You must increase and I must decrease. I now this moment, choose to lay my life down – to die to self and all of its fleshly facets. I honor You, LORD Jesus and Father, and joyfully bow in humility before Your Majesty. Grant Your enabling grace to my life, so I might please You in all things. I am crucified with Christ. I am dead, and my life is hid with Christ in God. Amen.*

Capture Points

1. Discuss John 12:24-26 and what it means to **"fall into the ground and die,"** as pertains to Christ and also all of those who would follow Him.

2. According to 1 Corinthians 15:1-4, what is **"the gospel"** that we stand in defined as? (KJV recommended)

3. What did Jesus tell us was the purpose for which He came? John 17:3

Chapter Two

The Essential Cross of Christ

"And, having made peace <u>through the blood of his cross</u>, by him to reconcile all things unto himself; by him, I say, whether they be things in earth, or things in heaven." Colossians 1:20

Mankind was separated from God due to his sin (Isa. 59:2). In order for man to be saved after his fall, it was essential for Christ to offer His perfect and sinless blood on the altar of the cross, a reality that had throughout Old Testament history been depicted and foreshadowed in the shedding of the blood of animals (Lev. 16-17; Heb. 10:1-22; 1 Pet. 1:18-19; Rev. 1:5). The **"seed of the woman (Messiah)"** had to be a sinless sacrificial offering, hence the virgin birth of the Son of God (Gen. 3:15; Matt. 1:18-23) – **"Therefore the Lord himself shall give you a sign; Behold, a virgin shall conceive, and bear a son, and shall call his name Immanuel (God with us)."** (Isa. 7:14) All men born after Adam were contaminated with sin and death, and therefore could not possibly bear a sinless child (Rom. 5:12). A divine Father was indispensable.

The sinless **"blood of his cross"** was the precious and sinless blood of redemption for all mankind (Col. 1:20; 1 Pet. 1:18-19).

> **"Forasmuch as ye know that ye were not redeemed with corruptible things, as silver and gold, from your vain conversation received by tradition from your fathers; But with the precious blood of Christ, as of a lamb without blemish and without spot." 1 Peter 1:18-19**

Of this sacrifice of our LORD Jesus Christ, James A. Fowler writes the following:

> "The death of Jesus Christ on a cross is an important truth of the Christian gospel. In fact, it is crucial to the gospel, the crux of the message, if we might employ additional English words derived from the Latin word *crux*, from which we also derive the English word 'cross.'
>
> The Greek word which we translate into English as 'cross' is *stauros*. *Stauros* originally indicated a pointed, vertical stake firmly fixed in the ground. The word was used for 'fence posts.' Later the word was used in the Greek language for a wooden stake fixed in the ground and used as an instrument of torture or death. The primary meaning of the word thus became a reference to an execution instrument comprised of wooden timbers and affixed in the ground." James A. Fowler, *The Blood of Christ*, www.ChristInYou.net/pages/crosschrst.html

Concerning the sacrificial death and blood of Christ, the spotless Lamb, and what it acquired, Fowler pens also these words:

> **"Propitiation.** The shed blood of Jesus in His sacrificial death was the objective satisfaction of God's death penalty for sin. 'God displayed Jesus as a propitiation in His blood' (Romans 3:25)." James A. Fowler *The Blood of Christ*, http://www.christinyou.net/pages/bloodchrst.html

The blessed hymn titled "There is a Fountain," by William Cowper, attempts to capture the beauty and blessedness of the myriad of glorious benefits purchased by the blood the Savior shed for sinners:

> "There is a fountain filled with blood, Drawn from Immanuel's veins, And sinners plunged beneath that flood, Lose all their guilty stains."

Though we know it to be true – because He told us, exactly how the sinless blood of redemption was imputed to sinful men is a mystery.

> "How Jesus transported His precious Blood from Calvary to heaven is not understood by mortal men, but the Scripture shows that He fulfilled the type, and therefore He must have sprinkled His own blood upon the mercy-seat (the throne of God) in heaven." H. A. Maxwell Whyte, *The Power of the Blood.* Springdale, Pa.: Whitaker House, pb, 1973, pg. 64

The blood of Christ's cross is what gives us access to the Father and all of His heavenly treasures, beginning with the gift of eternal life. The New Testament is a **"better covenant,"** procured by the blood of Jesus, who made possible that **"new and living way"** of accessing the Father and His divine favor. Because of Christ's priceless blood and what it obtained for us, born again saints can have complete confidence in approaching the **"throne of grace."** (Read Heb. 4:14-16 and rejoice!)

"Having therefore, brethren, boldness (confidence) to enter into the holiest by the blood of Jesus, By a new and living way, which he hath consecrated for us, through the veil, that is to say, his flesh." Hebrews 10:19-20

It is the blood of Jesus that has procured for us a relationship with God, and granted us the divine grace to walk in what Jesus taught is a **"daily"** cross we are to **"take up"** in following Him (Matt. 16:24-25; Lk. 9:23-24). Both **"the blood of his cross,"** and the daily experiential cross, are vital to the spiritual life. It is the atonement of the cross of Christ that makes possible the grace of God in the life of the rooted and overcoming saint – **"For the life of the flesh is in the blood: and I have given it to you upon the altar to make an atonement for your souls: for it is the blood that maketh an atonement for the soul."** (Lev. 17:11)

"For sin shall not have dominion over you: for ye are not under the law, but under grace." Romans 6:14

All born after Adam are born spiritually dead and separated from God by sin. We are all hopelessly separated from Him who is **"holy, holy, holy,"** until He draws us and we choose to respond to His divine influence upon our hearts and repent, placing all our trust in Christ (Isa. 6:3; Rev. 4:8). It is then that we are made new creatures in Christ, regenerated and given grace (divine enablement) to live pleasing to God.

Only the people who begin to realize just how depraved and wicked in heart they are, and how undeserving they are of divine mercy, can begin to appreciate the blood of the Savior. This must be a reality in our hearts and minds, lest we be puffed up unduly. This disciple loves to prayerfully and regularly speak this truth out found in Titus 3:

"For we ourselves also were sometimes foolish, disobedient, deceived, serving divers lusts and pleasures, living in malice and envy, hateful, and hating one another. But after that the kindness and love of God our Saviour toward man appeared, <u>Not by works of righteousness which we have done, but according to his mercy he saved us, by the washing of regeneration, and renewing of the Holy Ghost</u>; Which he shed on us abundantly through Jesus Christ our Saviour; That being justified by his grace, we should be made heirs according to the hope of eternal life." Titus 3:4-7

It is out of our own depravity and sinfulness that we are rescued by God's grace and saved into His eternal kingdom (Deut. 6:23-25; Ps. 40:1-3; Eph. 2:1-6; Col. 1:12-14). By this we are then made able to obey His will, pleasing Him in all things (Eph. 2:8-10). Those who have been saved and are presently walking with or abiding in Christ, are being perfected: He is working in them. They are **"his workmanship, created in Christ Jesus unto good works."** (Eph. 2:10) One thing is for sure: His workings in us are what matters first and foremost (Ps. 138:8; 1 Cor. 15:10; Phil. 1:6; 2:12-13). As we are given over to Him, He is working in us **"both to will and to do of his good pleasure."** (Phil. 2:12-13) When we are truly submitted, His grace-filled workings in us are shown in the works and fruit of our lives (1 Cor. 15:10; Eph. 2:8-10; 3:7; 4:7). Those who are truly His adore Him (Ps. 37:4). They delight in obeying Him whom they love (Ps. 40:8; Jn. 14:15, 21; 1 Jn. 2:3-5). Those who will remain in Christ to the end and be the overcomers who are blessed to dwell with Him forever, will be those who choose to love the LORD their God with all of their hearts, souls, minds, and strength – **"choose you this day whom ye will serve."** (Josh. 24:15)

As we trust Him fully, daily presenting ourselves living sacrifices to Him, we are made victorious overcomers in all things that glorify the LORD (Rom. 8:37; 12:12). This was all made possible by Christ's sacrifice, through which God poured out to us His priceless grace that brings us into His kingdom and enables us to walk with Him, pleasing in all things. Listen closely to Titus 2:11-12:

> **"For <u>the grace of God</u> that bringeth salvation hath appeared to all men, <u>Teaching us that, denying ungodliness and worldly lusts, we should live soberly, righteously, and godly, in this present world;</u>"**

The books of Romans and Hebrews clearly reveal to us that the law of Moses granted no victory over sin, and this is why the LORD replaced that inferior covenant with this **"better covenant"** and **"so great salvation"** purchased for us by Jesus' very blood (Heb. 2:3; 8:6).

> **"For the <u>law</u> was given by Moses, but <u>grace and truth</u> came by Jesus Christ." John 1:17**

The law of Moses was replaced by the **"grace and truth."**

> **"For what the law could not do, in that it was weak through the flesh, God sending his own Son in the likeness of sinful flesh, and for sin, condemned sin in the flesh: That the righteousness of the law might be fulfilled in us, who walk not after the flesh, but after the Spirit." Romans 8:3-4**

Now what is **"grace?"** What does it entail? *Grace* is defined as the divine influence upon the heart of the believer and the divine enablement in the life of that trusting saint. These definitions seem to be consistent with how the whole of Holy Scripture would qualify grace (in part).

Two Adams – Two Dispositions & Two Destinies

Speaking of the two Adams, the Scripture tells us:

"For since by man (Adam) came death, by man (Jesus) came also the resurrection of the dead. For as in Adam all die, even so in Christ shall all be made alive." I Corinthians 15:21, 22

All men are born in sin – after their natural progenitor, Adam, the first man. In that inherited state of spiritual death, natural man is separated from God, **"alienated from the life of God."** (Eph. 4:18). He has the disposition of depravity and wickedness (Gen. 6:5; Jer. 17:9; Rom. 3). Because of this, the Bible says: **"For there is not a just man upon earth, that doeth good, and sinneth not."** (Eccl. 7:20)

Of the two Adams and the natural and spiritual man, the Bible says this:

"And so it is written, The first man Adam was made a living soul; the last Adam was made a quickening (life-giving) spirit. Howbeit that was not first which is spiritual, but that which is natural; and afterward that which is spiritual. The first man is of the earth, earthy: the second man is the Lord from heaven (second Adam). As is the earthy, such are they also that are earthy: and as is the heavenly, such are they also that are heavenly. And as we have borne the image of the earthy, we (the saved) shall also bear the image of the heavenly. Now this I say, brethren, that flesh and blood cannot inherit the kingdom of God; neither doth corruption inherit incorruption." 1 Corinthians 15:45-50

Jesus is the second Adam and **"quickening spirit"** and **"life"** who breathes spiritual life into all who repent and believe, as He translates them into His kingdom, causing them to pass from spiritual death to spiritual life (Jn. 1:4; 5:24; 14:6; 1 Cor. 15:45; 1 Jn. 3:14; 5:12).

> **"Verily, verily, I say unto you, He that heareth my word, and believeth on him that sent me, hath everlasting life, and shall not come into condemnation; but is passed from death unto life." John 5:24**

Any person outside of Jesus Christ is in spiritual death and darkness. God the Father plainly and repeatedly told us that the possibility and surety of pleasing Him was exclusively wrapped up in knowing His Son – the One in whom He is **"well pleased."** (Matt. 3:17; 12:18; 17:5; 2 Pet. 1:17, etc.)

> **"And lo a voice from heaven, saying, This is my beloved Son, in whom I am well pleased." Matthew 3:17**

> **"He that hath the Son hath life; and he that hath not the Son of God hath not life." 1 John 5:12** (Do you have this one memorized yet?)

Of Jesus Christ, the Bible says: **"Who was delivered for our offences, and was raised again for our justification."** (Rom. 4:25)

How did Paul **"die daily"**? He sentenced himself to death, kept under his body of sin, and was crucified with Christ to the world and the world to him (Gal. 2:20; 6:14). In this God's grace was overwhelmingly sufficient, granting the victory made possible only by the grace of God provided to us in the blood of Jesus (2 Cor. 12:9-10).

Taking up the cross to follow the Savior who bled is a command, and for good reason, considering that which can be understood from the message of Holy Scripture. The perfection of Christ should become a lived-out reality – manifested – in the lives of all whom He has purchased (2 Cor. 4:10-11). This can only happen by His enabling grace, Holy Spirit, and a continual **"bearing about in the body**

the dying of the Lord Jesus." All that are His are not their own, but bought with the price of His blood (1 Cor. 6:19-20).

In the biblical picture, the saved person's point of initial salvation is only the beginning of his participatory life in the Gospel with the LORD, who bled to buy him back from sin and the wrath to come. His moment of being brought into the kingdom is merely the starting point of his daily, ongoing partaking in the Gospel – the death, burial, and resurrection life of Christ. The genuine disciple of Jesus never outgrows his need for participating with Christ in the Gospel. The **"Gospel ... is the power of God unto salvation to every one that believeth."** (Rom. 1:16) The true disciple follows Christ **"daily,"** and that includes denying himself so that Jesus can reign in his mortal body (2 Cor. 4:10-11). The person who truly loves the LORD, chooses to obediently delight in daily abstaining from serving self-interests so that he can serve Jesus (Lk. 9:23-24). In daily participation with Christ in His Gospel, the disciple is **"raised up"** in the power of the Spirit to fully please God (Rom. 8:11).

We *must* suffer. We must suffer the death of sin and self, and all those who do – *only* those who do – will be raised up and blessed to be overcomers, who will one day dwell in that New Jerusalem (Rev. 3:5; 21:7).

There is no way to become regenerate outside of the blood of Jesus, which deals with the sinful nature in regeneration (Jn. 1:12-13; 5:24; 2 Cor. 5:17-18; Tit. 3:5-7; 1 Jn. 3:14). Divine **"propitiation"** creates a new man who is empowered to live powerfully pleasing to God – if he lives by faith in the Spirit (Rom. 3:25; 5:17-21; 6:14; 8:1-14; 2 Cor. 5:17-18; Eph. 4:22-24; 1 Jn. 2:2).

Christ shed His perfect blood on the cross to atone for mankind's sins, and to redeem and forgive sinners (Col.

1:14). Additionally, His atoning death released divine grace for overcoming victory over all sin, for all who will take seriously His command, **"If any man will come after me, let him deny himself, and take up his cross, and follow me."** (Matt. 16:24; Heb. 4:14-16) The cross was an execution instrument the Savior bled upon. When taken up by believers, the cross is an instrument of death to the sinful nature and defiling sins of the body, that the power of God might triumph in magnificent victory in their daily personal lives (Mk. 7:20-23; 2 Cor. 4:10-12, 14; Gal. 2:20; 6:14).

After the fall of man in the Garden of creation, the claims of divine justice were only satisfied by the offering of the spotless Lamb of God (Lev. 16-17; Jn. 1:29). This blessed offering is what allows men the opportunity and privilege to come to God. Heaven's salvation is wrapped up in one Person – Jesus Christ, the Son of God.

> **"For there is one God, and one mediator between God and men, the man Christ Jesus." 1 Timothy 2:5**

> **"Neither is there salvation in any other: for there is none other name under heaven given among men, whereby we must be saved." Acts 4:12**

Christ stated:

> **"I am <u>the</u> way ... no man cometh to the Father but by me." John 14:6**

PRAYER: *Father, thank You kindly for sending Your only begotten Son for me – for all my sins. I am not my own but rather bought with the price of Your blood, Jesus. My life is no longer my own but Yours. I am all yours and You are all mine. This moment I am asking you to multiply Your grace to my life and fill me afresh with Your Holy Spirit. I want to know You more and be blessed to be conformed to Your holy image. Amen.*

Capture Points

1. What was man's dilemma that Christ came to solve? Genesis 6:5, 12; Isaiah 59:2; Jeremiah 17:9; and Romans 6:23

2. Enjoy a triumphal discussion of the sole solution God provided for man's core problem and dilemma by sending His only begotten Son. Examine the following Scriptures in this dialogue: Matthew 26:28; 2 Corinthians 5:19; Colossians 1:14, 20; 1 Timothy 1:15; Hebrews 9:22; 1 Peter 1:18-19; and Revelation 1:5 (KJV recommended)

3. Transcribe 1 John 5:12 onto an index card: **"He that hath the Son hath life; and he that hath not the Son of God hath not life."** (KJV)

Chapter Three

The Essential Cross of the Believer

**"For whosoever will save his life shall lose it ... "
Matthew 16:25**

Now that we know who the Way is – Jesus, let's look into what this very Son of God Himself said concerning those who would follow Him. After all, if a person is going to go to God's Heaven, he needs to find out what God Himself said is essential to get there, right?

> **"Then said Jesus unto his disciples, If ANY man will come after me, let him deny himself, and take up his cross, and follow me. For whosoever will save his life shall lose it: and whosoever will lose his life for my sake shall find it. For what is a man profited, if he shall gain the whole world, and lose his own soul? or what shall a man give in exchange for his soul?" Matthew 16:24-26**

Like it or not, Jesus is speaking here of the eternal soul of every man. If need be, read His words again here. Notice that the Son of God uses the terms **"if ANY man"** and **"whosoever."** Jesus is speaking to all about His requirements and conditions. (Anybody want to argue with the Son of God?) Did you notice that there is no special privilege or concession given out here for those who have previously been saved? We should rid our minds of the subtle deception that we are somehow "secure" outside of the protection that comes from obedience to God's Word (Prov. 30:5; Acts 20:32). Only those who are not currently **"doers"** of the Word of God are deceived into thinking they are secure while not presently abiding in Christ.

> **"But be ye doers of the word, and not hearers only, deceiving your own selves." James 1:22**

The apostle Paul said, **"I die daily."** (1 Cor. 15:31) How did Paul **"die daily"**? How is this exemplary apostle's dying depicted in Scripture? He sentenced himself to death, kept under his body of sin, and was crucified with Christ and to the world, and the world to him. He was buried with Christ, and determined to glory in Christ's cross alone (Rom. 6:3-4; 1 Cor. 9:27; 2 Cor. 1:9; Gal. 2:20; 6:14).

We were all born in sin and **"dead in sins,"** and now the LORD **"hath quickened us (made us alive) together with Christ."** (Rom. 6:8; Eph. 2:5) After being found and saved by the LORD, the believer should follow Christ in water baptism, yet only to show that he is now **"dead with Christ"** and that Christ now reigns in his life, as he is now **"raised up"** with Christ (Rom. 6:3-4; 8:11). Water baptism is the public announcement showing and openly declaring one's own death, burial, and resurrection with Christ, one's new Master. The death of self is symbolized in the going down into the water, and the coming up out of the water represents the resurrection accomplished by Jesus and now made effectual in that life. The Gospel is not about H2O, but rather it's about being baptized into Christ's death – being dead, buried, and raised up with Him (Rom. 6:3-4; Col. 2:11-12). As we are dead with Christ and to self, buried with Him, He raises us up in His power to please Him.

One's entrance into the kingdom of God at his initial salvation is only the beginning point of his participation in the Gospel – the death, burial, and resurrection life of Christ. One never outgrows his essential need for the participating with Jesus in the Gospel. The true disciple follows Christ **"daily,"** and that includes denying himself and taking up his cross to be crucified with his LORD and Savior. He chooses Christ who is the life, the only way, and the truth; and is therefore ready for His soon return.

> **"When Christ, who is our life, shall appear, then shall ye also appear with him in glory." Colossians 3:4**

Romans 6 is not speaking of water baptism, but it is that which is signified or symbolized by water baptism – being dead to self and sin, buried with Christ, and raised up to new life with Jesus, to no longer serve sin and please self but Christ. Look at verse 4 of Romans 6:

> **"Therefore we are buried with him by baptism into death: that like as Christ was raised up from the dead by the glory of the Father, even so we also should walk in newness of life."**

Note the words of Holy Scripture here – **"buried ... death ... raised up."** This is the Gospel as it is being lived out in our lives. As we choose to daily die – moment by moment – giving way to His greater purpose, He raises us up out of the place of death and burial to be led and used of Him.

Anointed to the Burial

I remember fondly the days leading up to my water baptism as a young believer. My pastor at the time was keenly aware of the importance of people understanding what water baptism is, so he gave me a question and answer type work sheet to go through. Each question gave Scriptures to study and get the answers from. So, when I was water baptized there was a realization and spiritual anointing that came upon me – a distinct sealing type phenomenon by the Holy Spirit in which I was buried or hid with Christ in God. There was clearly a work of the Holy Spirit that day. Beloved, there is no power or magic in water. God is trying to get at death to self, and His Spirit enables such. Water baptism merely represents the going down into death process, and coming up out of the water represents the raised up life. Without the work of the divine Person of the Holy Ghost and the believer's going down into the death of Christ, water baptism is futile.

It is the work of the Spirit of God that is essential in our new birth, death, burial, and resurrection, just as He participated in our LORD's birth, death, burial, and resurrection (Lk. 1:35; Rom. 8:11; Col. 2:11-12).

> **"For to this end (for this chief purpose) Christ both died, and rose, and revived, that he might be Lord both of the dead and living." Romans 14:9**

Not only is the Holy Spirit's involvement and Jesus Christ's sacrifice on His cross essential - where He worked with Christ to shed His blood to redeem us - but according to this same and only Savior, the taking up the cross to deny and bury self is also essential in pleasing God. His resurrection rule cannot occur without the willing participation of the recipient of His salvation. Jesus died to buy us back from sin, Satan, and slavery to self; and now our lives are made new in Him, all things now being of God and under Christ's reign (Rom. 14:9; 2 Cor. 5:17-18).

> **"And that he died for all, that they which live should not henceforth live unto themselves, but unto him which died for them, and rose again." 2 Corinthians 5:15**

Those redeemed by the One who bled on that cross that stood atop Calvary's hill, should from the moment they are grafted in, no longer serve self but the Savior.

The way the believer lives unto (pleases) the LORD and not self, is by the power of the One who was for us **"slain from the foundation of the world."**

> **"And all that dwell upon the earth shall worship him (the antichrist), whose names are not written in the book of life of the Lamb slain from the foundation of the world." Revelation 13:8**

It all began **"from the foundation of the world"** when in His mind, **"God so loved the world that he gave his only begotten Son."** (Jn. 3:16; Rom. 5:6, 8) So, redemption through **"the Lamb slain,"** which grants His overcoming grace, began in the mind of God from **"the foundation of the world."** (Jer. 1:5; Rev. 13:8) How could we ever now doubt how much He loves us! It is to Him alone who is worthy that we, with our lives, now give **"honour, and glory, and blessing."**

> **"Saying with a loud voice, Worthy is the Lamb that was slain to receive power, and riches, and wisdom, and strength, and honour, and glory, and blessing." Revelation 5:12**

All this being said, we should observe that God doesn't do things against the free-moral agency He gave to every man. The individual must be **"willing and obedient"** if he is to **"eat the good of the land."** (Isa. 1:19-20)

> "Gaze, oh gaze on the divine form, the eternal glory, the heavenly beauty, the tenderly pleading gentleness of crucified love, as it stretches out its pierced hands and says, 'Oh, will you not abide with me?'" Andrew Murray, *Abide in Christ*, p. 175

"The New Man"

> "That ye put off concerning the former conversation the old man, which is corrupt according to the deceitful lusts; And be renewed in the spirit of your mind; And that ye put on the new man, which after God is created in righteousness and true holiness." Ephesians 4:22-24

You are no longer your own, but rather bought with a price (1 Cor. 6:19-20).

If a saint chooses not to live out of the **"new man, which after God is created in righteousness and true holiness,"** he will by default revert back to the Adamic nature and its sinful deeds. Is this permissible in God's eyes? Does the LORD overlook the sins of those He has saved?

> "What shall we say then? <u>Shall we continue in sin, that grace may abound? God forbid</u>. How shall we, that are dead to sin, live any longer therein? Know ye not, that so many of us as were baptized into Jesus Christ were baptized into his death? Therefore we are buried with him by baptism into death: that like as Christ was raised up from the dead by the glory of the Father, even so we also should walk in newness of life. For if we have been planted together in the likeness of his death, we shall be also in the likeness of his resurrection: Knowing this, that our old man is crucified with him, that the body of sin might be destroyed, that henceforth we should not serve sin. <u>For he that is dead is freed from sin</u>. Now if we be dead with Christ, we believe that we shall also live with him:" Romans 6:1-8

The "But" Factor

The taking up of the cross, the implement of death to self, is essential in separating the saint from the taint of sin, self, and Satan, which would otherwise defile us in the eyes of Him who is **"holy, holy, holy."** (Isa. 6:3; Rev. 4:8)

Are you beginning to see why the cross is essential – both Christ's and ours? The LORD told His own covenant people that their sins had separated them from Him.

> **"But <u>your iniquities have separated between you and your God</u>, and your sins have hid his face from you, that he will not hear." Isaiah 59:2**

The word **"but"** here speaks of the dividing factor or attribute of sin. Sin interrupts our fellowship with Him who is holy. Sin still separates. Both the cross of Jesus (first and foremost) and our carrying our own cross deal with the problem of sin, but only when applied and participated in.

To take up the cross in obedience to Christ's command is to agree with God that the sinful man must be mortified with his evil deeds and desires (Gal. 5:24). When one takes up his cross, which is the implement of death to self, he demonstrates that he loves the LORD more than self. God then blesses his life to be separate from sin and sinners, and to escape the taint of sin that would otherwise defile him in the eyes of Him who is **"holy, holy, holy."** (Isa. 6:3; Rev. 4:8) Such a work is essential to separate the saint from the stain of sin, self, and Satan. The cross makes possible both one's death to self and sin, and the resurrection presence of God (Rom. 6:7; 2 Cor. 4:10-11). Holy Spirit enabled death to self disallows, stifles, and restrains the work of sin in us so that Christ's divine life might work in and through us to bless others (Rom. 8:13; 2 Cor. 4:12).

Any person who has been made righteous by the LORD and now somehow believes he is secure while living in sin, is utterly deceived and all of Scripture testifies to this truth.

Who is it that is made free from the sins that violate the holiness of the LORD? – **"For he that is dead is freed from sin."** (Rom. 6:7)

Beloved, it is the sanctifying work of the cross of Jesus and the application of it in the life of the saint that sets him apart in holiness to the Savior.

We find not one promise of security or assurance in Holy Scripture given to any person who is not presently abiding in Jesus Christ – as He prescribed in His Word (Jn. 10:27-29; 15:1-6). Jesus promised His original 12 apostles an eternal throne in Heaven, yet 1 of them chose not to abide or remain in Him, and subsequently went to hell for his iniquity (Acts 1:25). Christ promised His 12 that **"ye shall be hated of all men for my name's sake: but he that endureth to the end shall be saved."** (Matt. 10:22) Remaining in Christ – enduring to the end of one's life – is a divinely-issued condition for being with the LORD eternally (this Bible subject is covered extensively in the book titled *Lie of the Ages,* which can be seen at www.SafeGuardYourSoul.com).

Concerning the daily cross and how it applies and does not apply to the believer, David Kupelian, vice president and managing editor of *WorldNetDaily.com,* writes:

> "It's self-evident that we're all born with a troublesome nature called 'pride.' Basically, pride is the part of us that wants to be God. It loves being praised, quickly puffs up with angry judgment over the real or perceived wrongs of others – and as a rule is oblivious to its own faults. Moreover, you can think of pride as a 'life form' – a living, breathing 'something' which,

like any other life form or 'creature,' can be fed or starved. When it's fed, it grows and enlarges; when it is starved, it diminishes and dies – daily.

Of course – and this is something of a divine paradox – as Christians, we know we can't save ourselves, and yet we are most definitely called to obedience. So, let's not slough off our responsibility to 'die daily' by comfortably presuming on the unending mercy of God. His mercy is unending, indeed, but also balanced with justice, and these two seemingly contradictory qualities work together mysteriously and wonderfully toward our redemption, but only in the truly sincere human soul that doesn't tempt God."

This writer realizes that the modern gospel differs from this biblical truth and message, but whom shall we trust? God, or mere men? Who is the Judge before whom we will one day stand to give account?

"Let God be true and every man a liar." Romans 3:4

May God bless each of us to **"Let God be true and every man a liar,"** placing Him and therefore His holy truth above the words, concepts, or philosophies of any other (Prov. 21:30).

Do we take God at His Word? Do we believe, trust, embrace, and obey His words?

> "The vigour of our spiritual life will be in exact proportion to the place held by the Bible in our life and thoughts." George Mueller

After repenting and receiving Christ and initial salvation, one must remain in fellowship with (abide in) Jesus till the end of his life or he will lose out eternally (Matt. 10:22;

24:13; Rom. 11:22; Col. 1:23; Heb. 2:3, 3:6, 12-15; 10:26-39; 12:14-15; Rev. 2-3, etc.). Jesus told those who had believed that if they continued in His Word (not man's) they would be His disciples, and that they would know the truth and the truth would make them free (Jn. 8:31-32).

Jesus died to justify us, saving us from living in sin which would merit us the wrath of God (Rom. 5:9). He certainly didn't die to grant us a license to live in sin, but rather grace and power over sin (Rom. 6; Tit. 2:11-12).

The deeds of the body must be put to death or they will wreak sinful havoc on that life. The cross is the only answer, not behavioral modification, which is the level on which most messages seek to deal with sin. If the sinful nature is allowed to reign by not being put down, the course of inherited iniquity will be sin and death (Rom. 6:1-23; James 1:14-15).

> **"For if ye live after the flesh, ye shall die (spiritual death – separation): but if ye through the Spirit do mortify the deeds of the body, ye shall live." Romans 8:13**

When man fell in the Garden, he became dead inside. He lost the relationship and place of intimacy with His Maker, and no longer needed to be tempted externally. Man's original inner inclination toward the LORD became slanted and tending toward self. He became self-absorbed instead of absorbed into the LORD his Maker. He then lived unto self – out of self. His inward bent is now to please self, which is rebellion and part and parcel of the first Adam. This is the fate of all born with the stain of inherent sin.

Man cannot please God in his fallen nature – **"Because the carnal mind is enmity against God."** (Rom. 8:7) This is why fallen man must be regenerated, and thereafter self must be denied by the power and grace of the Holy Ghost (Rom. 8:13; Tit. 3:5-7). When self will is laid down flat and the LORD's will takes over, victory is brought about – **"For sin shall not have dominion over you: for ye are not under the law, but under grace."** (Rom. 6:14) God's greater grace, will, and glory override self and succeed triumphantly. He said we are **"more than conquerors through him that loved us."** (Rom. 8:37) It's only *when* and *as* self is laid down and sacrificed that the far exceeding blessing of the life of Jesus is manifested (2 Cor. 4:10-11). When out of self and in Christ, the saint is pleasing to the Father. Remember that it is only in Jesus Christ that the Father told us He is **"well pleased."** (Matt. 3:17; 12:18; 17:5). To be in Christ is to be pleasing to the Father, but to be in self is to be at enmity with Him (Rom. 8:1-7). May His divine life engulf us today as He increases and we decrease (Jn. 3:30). **"But thanks be to God, which giveth us the victory through our Lord Jesus Christ."** (1 Cor. 15:57)

The Bible calls our fallen sinful nature the **"flesh," "body of sin," "carnal,"** and the **"old man."** We are told to crucify the old man that is bent toward sin and evil desires that if acted upon, would cause us to be in violation against the holiness of God (Gal. 5:24). God is holy; therefore that fallen, sinful nature must be subdued, or one will not be pleasing to the LORD but rather experience spiritual **"death."** (Rom. 8:6, 13) The Bible tells us that **"the flesh"** is **"at enmity against God."** (Rom. 8:7, 13) The apostle Paul said he had to **"keep under"** his sinful nature so that he would not ultimately become a **"castaway."** (1 Cor. 9:27) Sound out this word **"castaway."** Many today would seek to manipulate the meaning of this word to fit their own convoluted theology, yet a **"castaway"** is simply one who would be cast away from God and forfeit His eternal blessings due to a violation of His order and holiness.

> **"For to be carnally minded is death; but to be spiritually minded is life and peace. Because the carnal mind is enmity against God: for it is not**

subject to the law of God, neither indeed can be. So then they that are in the flesh cannot please God." Romans 8:6-8

The sin of Adam affected the whole world. It was a sin that was felt throughout God's creation, which was before according to His pristine and perfect design (Gen. 1-3). Adam's sin affected all human beings from the time of his transgression. Many call this the doctrine of *Inherent Sin,* which states that Adam's sin nature was passed on to all who came after him (Rom. 5:12).

"Wherefore, as by one man sin entered into the world, and death by sin; and so death passed upon all men, for that all have sinned." Romans 5:12

Once the LORD finds and regenerates the individual saint, this universally inherited Adamic nature must be restrained or made unresponsive by the power of the Holy Spirit and the willing participation of the disciple, in order for the life of Christ to manifest in that life – "if ye through the Spirit do mortify the deeds of the body, ye shall live." (Rom. 8:13)

In the same way that we inherit physical features from our parents and ancestors, each and every man has inherited from Adam his fallen spiritual nature and condition, which is spiritual death – "death passed upon all men." (Rom. 5:12) All men are born of water spiritually dead (separated from and at enmity with God).

Since each and every human born after Adam inherited his sinful nature and spiritual condition, he is also under the condemnation of God. We all stand guilty before God and deserving of the punishment of our sin.

No More Condemnation

> **"There is therefore now no condemnation to them which are in Christ Jesus, who walk not after the flesh, but after the Spirit." Romans 8:1**

According to Romans 8:1, there is an initial and an ongoing condition for getting out from under the **"condemnation"** of God:

- One must repent, believe upon, and be **"in Christ Jesus,"** and

- **"walk not after the flesh, but after the Spirit."**

Remaining or abiding in Christ is essential to remaining in the justification and blessing of God (see also John 15:1-6).

"There is therefore now no condemnation to them which are in Christ Jesus" - so as long as the redeemed believer remains **"in Christ Jesus,"** he is not under **"condemnation."** (Rom. 8:1)

"No good thing" dwells in man outside of Christ, and as long as he remains out of Christ, he is a slave to corruption (Rom. 6-8). See Romans 7:18. The only victory is Christ and being in Him. Only Jesus can conquer sin, and those who are in Him are possessed with the power of His conquering, overcoming grace.

The first Adam was conquered by sin. The second Adam (Jesus) conquered sin (Rom. 5). The first Adam left us with an inherent nature of sin while the second Adam regenerates, redeems, and rescues us from the sinful nature, condemnation, penalty, and punishment we received from the first Adam.

> **"But not as the offence, so also is the free gift. For if through the offence of one many be dead, much more the grace of God, and the gift by grace, which is by one man, Jesus Christ, hath abounded unto many.**

And not as it was by one that sinned, so is the gift: for the judgment was by one to condemnation, but the free gift is of many offences unto justification. For if by one man's offence death reigned by one; much more they which receive abundance of grace and of the gift of righteousness shall reign in life by one, Jesus Christ.) Therefore as by the offence of one judgment came upon all men to condemnation; even so by the righteousness of one the free gift came upon all men unto justification of life. For as by one man's disobedience many were made sinners, so by the obedience of one shall many be made righteous. Moreover the law entered, that the offence might abound. But where sin abounded, grace did much more abound: That as sin hath reigned unto death, even so might grace reign through righteousness unto eternal life by Jesus Christ our Lord." Romans 5:15-21**

"But where sin abounded, grace did much more abound." Through Jesus Christ, the Church and the individual believer have been granted **"great grace"** to live according to the righteous standards of the One who told us He is **"holy, holy, holy."** (Isa. 6:3; Acts 4:33; Rev. 4:8) Grace was given to grant the believer power over sin and not to justify him in his sin (Tit. 2:11-12). When we come before His throne of grace, it is not only to receive mercy, but also grace, or divine enablement, to overcome (Heb. 4:16; Rev. 2-3). Fighting the good fight of faith and overcoming are a must (1 Tim. 6:12; Rev. 2-3).

> **"Let every one that nameth the name of Christ depart from iniquity." 2 Timothy 2:19**

The opposite of living in sin is living in the place of holiness. We are **"called"** and commanded to live holy, and this should be of concern to every person who **"nameth the name of Christ."** (2 Tim. 2:19)

> **"But as he which hath called you is holy, so be ye holy in all manner of conversation; Because it is written, Be ye holy; for I am holy." 1 Peter 1:15-16**

His holiness prevails, and sin cannot have dominion over those who are dead with Christ, buried, and presently raised up in His life. This is the fully-orbed truth expressed in the whole of this passage.

Derek Tidball, in his book *The Message of the Cross* asks:

> "Why is there an uneasy silence about crucifying the sinful nature with its passions when it is clearly so crucial to the Bible's teaching about holiness? For all our excuses, the truth is perhaps that such teaching does not fit easily into a comfortable world where self-indulgence and self-satisfaction reign supreme. Our silence betrays how deeply the atmosphere of the world has infected the church, and how we fear the opinion of the world more than the opinion of the Lord. The cross, however, cannot be shunted to the sidelines. It stands high on the hill of Calvary and calls individual believers to stand apart from the cultural values of the world. It equally calls the church as a whole to a deep repentance for its compromise with the world, to take radical action in ejecting sin from its midst and to demonstrate a new seriousness about holiness." pp. 240-241

Many writers of old and today read Romans 5 and ignore the divinely-imposed conditions of Romans 6. They therefore come out with a slanted and dangerous theology, which has led many to **"turn(ing) the grace of God into lasciviousness (license for sin)."** (Jude 3-4)

49

Always remember that without personal holiness, no man is going to see the LORD (Matt. 5:8; Heb. 12:14; Rev. 3:5-6).

If one only read this portion of Scripture (Romans 5), he might lean toward Calvinism and an unconditional eternal security, yet there's more to this picture, and the ensuing verses reveal the rest of the story. Romans 6 reveals the God-given personal responsibility of each saved saint, and how these blessings of His grace are conditional upon the obedience of the individual recipient. (Read Romans 6-8 through 3 times in the next week.)

A thorough and ongoing look at Romans chapters 3-8 is essential to a sound doctrinal foundation.

The apostle Paul said:

> **"For I know that in me (that is, in my flesh,) dwelleth no good thing: for to will is present with me; but how to perform that which is good I find not." Romans 7:18**

We must rightly – biblically – assess our true spiritual nature, and when we do, we will know that without Jesus, we are corrupt and depraved in the nature of the first Adam. Knowing that there is **"no good thing"** that dwells in us, that is, in our flesh, we should sentence our self-life to death, that our lives might rely upon the LORD and not sinful self.

> **"But <u>we had the sentence of death in ourselves</u>, that we should not trust in ourselves, but in God which raiseth the dead." 2 Corinthians 1:9**

The lack of teaching in the Christian world on this all-important biblical truth has greatly hindered the understanding of many who have a desire to fully please and serve the LORD. May the LORD bless each of us to have this message of the cross embedded deeply into our hearts and minds. Speaking of His own cross, Jesus told His disciples to **"Let these sayings sink down into your ears: for the Son of man shall be delivered into the hands of men."** (Lk. 9:44)

The gross lack of attention to this core biblical truth has given way to a myriad of Cain-type methods to modify behavior instead of teaching men to crucify the evil tendencies of the fallen nature and walk in the new man – presenting ourselves as living sacrifices unto the LORD, and being transformed by the renewing of our minds (Rom. 12:1-2).

PRAYER: *LORD, please teach me Your truth. Allow my heart and mind to understand from whence I came and where You desire to take this life You gave. I am sinful by nature and yet, You have made me a new creature in Christ, granting Your overcoming grace by the power of Your Spirit. Right this moment, if never before, I humble myself under Your mighty hand, fully submitting my life to You, begging You to live in me and raise my life up to glorify You alone from this moment forward. I am dead and buried with Christ – crucified with Christ. I am dead and my life is hid with Christ in God. Holy Father, into Your hands I commend my spirit. Amen.*

Capture Points

1. On an index card, write out the words of Jesus recorded in Matthew 16:24-26.

2. Examining the words of Romans 8:13-14, discuss the role of the Holy Spirit in empowering and leading the disciple to glorify God in this life by putting away the works of the flesh and living a life in the Spirit (KJV recommended).

3. Because there is **"no good thing"** that dwells in us (in our flesh), discuss practical measures as to how the disciple of Jesus is to daily sentence to death the deeds of the sinful nature (Romans 7:18; 2 Corinthians 1:9; Galatians 5:19-21).

Chapter Four

The Daily Cross in Prayer

**"My voice shalt thou hear in the morning, O LORD;
in the morning will I direct *my prayer* unto thee,
and will look up." Psalms 5:3**

Let's isolate and dismantle these words of God a bit. Under
the direct inspiration of the Holy Spirit, David says to the
LORD:

- That He (God) would hear his (David's) **"voice"**

- That **"in the morning"** the Psalmist would arise and
  seek God in prayer

- Deliberately **"in the morning,"** he would **"direct"**
  his prayer and praying to the LORD

- **"in the morning ... I will look up"**

From this passage, we see that David planned or scheduled,
in an intentional and calculated fashion, to meet with the
LORD every morning. The phrase **"in the morning"** appears
twice in this inspired transmission of the Holy Ghost. The
man whose heart panted after the LORD – to behold His
precious beauty – declared that he would **"direct"** (point)

his prayer upward to the LORD **"in the morning."** (Ps. 5:3; 27:4; Acts 13:22) Communing with the LORD was priority to David, and therefore occupied first place in his daily life. He sought the LORD firstly as he arose from sleep, and before he went forth into his day.

Jesus commanded that if any person will come after Him – truly follow Him – he must deny himself, take up his cross, and follow Him (Lk. 9:23-24). There is no place that the cross applies more than in daily prayer. The moment one arises, he will choose either to seek God or dwell upon self-sentiments and such. He will seek Christ, or he will seek his own salvation or rescue from his troubles. We all make a **"daily"** choice:

> **"... choose you this day whom ye will serve; whether the gods which your fathers served that *were* on the other side of the flood, or the gods of the Amorites, in whose land ye dwell: <u>but as for me and my house, we will serve the LORD</u>." Joshua 24:15**

No different from those covenant saints the LORD spoke to in this important passage, those whom we dwell among are serving self – the flesh – and yet we are called upon by the LORD to **"choose"** to daily serve Him rather than self. We are called to **"be blameless and harmless, the sons of God, without rebuke, in the midst of a crooked and perverse nation, among whom ye shine as lights in the world; Holding forth the word of life."** (Phil. 2:15-16)

The LORD is calling us to purposefully declare Him as the LORD and Master of our lives, and this we do by making the premeditated decision to seek Him daily in prayer communion. Like Joshua, the way we **"choose"** to **"serve"** God must be premeditated, deliberate, daily, and in practicality. Daily, early morning, first fruit prayer is all three of these. It is the fruit of the crucified life – the life that is dead to self and in whom Christ dwells and reigns. – **"Ye are dead and your life is hid with Christ in God."** (Col. 3:3)

To those who seek God and not their own devices, there are many benefits (Ps. 68:19).

> **"Be careful for nothing; but in every thing by prayer and supplication with thanksgiving let your requests be made known unto God. And the peace of God, which passeth all understanding, shall keep your hearts and minds through Christ Jesus." Philippians 4:6-7**

The precious peace of the **"Prince of Peace"** rules and reigns and makes sound the hearts of those who deny self's ability to overcome and solve issues and problems, and instead earnestly and diligently rely upon God's power to do such for them (Isa. 9:6; 26:3).

> **"Thou wilt keep *him* in perfect peace, *whose* mind *is* stayed *on thee*: because he trusteth in thee. Trust ye in the LORD for ever: for in the LORD JEHOVAH *is* everlasting strength." Isaiah 26:3-4**

As we center our whole being upon Jesus Christ, our thoughts will be upward to His **"glorious high throne,"** which is **"the place of our sanctuary."** (Jer. 17:12)

God is calling each of His saints to center his whole being on those things that **"are true, whatsoever things *are* honest, whatsoever things *are* just, whatsoever things *are* pure, whatsoever things *are* lovely, whatsoever things *are* of good report; if *there be* any virtue, and if *there be* any praise, think on these things."** (Phil. 4:8)

So, according to Philippians 4:6-8, saints are to rely upon the LORD and not self by submitting all their requests in prayer to Him who is their Source, and to think upon those things of Christ which are **"true ... honest ... just ... pure ... lovely ... of good report ... if** *there be* **any virtue ... if** *there be* **any praise."** It is **"these things"** that we are instructed to **"think on."** (Phil. 4:8)

God's thoughts are infinitely higher than ours, and yet it is not until we become truly **"crucified with Christ"** that we are going to be ruled by His thoughts and peace (Isa. 55:8-9; Gal. 2:20; Phil. 4:6-7).

Changing the way one thinks is being done by millions of people who are not regenerated (not born again). New Age and religious teachers hold this thought transformation teaching closely. Anyone can change the way they think for self-serving reasons – to stop smoking, to visualize and earn more money, to have more self-esteem, etc. However, hell still awaits all who are not born again, and that takes facing the living God and Judge in repentance for sin and placing all faith in Jesus Christ, the only Savior (Acts 4:12; 1 Tim. 2:5). The only renewing of the mind and thoughts that brings glory to Jesus Christ, is that which begins with one casting his whole being upon the LORD afresh – presenting himself a **"living sacrifice ... unto God."** Let's look at Romans 12:

> **"I beseech you therefore, brethren, by the mercies of God, that ye present your bodies a living sacrifice, holy, acceptable unto God,** *which is* **your reasonable service. And be not conformed to this world: but be ye transformed by the renewing of your mind, that ye may prove what** *is* **that good, and acceptable, and perfect, will of God." Romans 12:1-2**

Those who are presenting their bodies to the LORD as **"living sacrifice(s)"** are infused and enabled by His grace to keep their minds or thoughts stayed (fixed) upon the LORD and not self, as they look for Jesus' soon return (Col. 3:1-4). They trust Christ and not their own strength, reasoning, whims, philosophies, or wisdom. As they give themselves over to Christ and His infinite divine power, and become weak in self and self's abilities, Jesus' power raises them up to trust Him and rely upon Him alone – to rest the weight of their whole beings in Him who is able. They first declare that they are not able, and that only **"God is able."** (Eph. 3:20; 2 Cor. 9:8) These are they who have and are finding out in a personal way that there really is nothing impossible with the LORD!

> **"And Jesus looking upon them saith, <u>With men *it is* impossible, but not with God: for with God all things are possible</u>." Mark 10:27**

Abraham trusted God. He is our human example of a man who walked with God – by faith believing that God would raise up that to which he died. Concerning the promise of a son being born to him and his aged wife, the Bible records these words from the LORD to His servant Abraham:

> **"Is any thing too hard for the LORD? At the time appointed I will return unto thee, according to the time of life, and Sarah shall have a son." Genesis 18:14**

If God can and will split the Red Sea for His people, and cause a 100-year-old man and his 90-year-old wife to have a child, what in your life can't He do? (Gen. 17:17)

Here's yet another question posed to our hearts from the LORD:

> **"Behold, I *am* the LORD, the God of all flesh: <u>is there any thing too hard for me?</u>" Jeremiah 32:27**

God requires that we die to self-will, self-help, and self-esteem, and lay our lives in His holy, perfect, and more-than-sufficient hands. He can then work in us and in our lives – raising up His holy standard and power to glorify Himself in and through His children. Nothing will be impossible for the LORD to perform in the lives of those who deny themselves and, like Abraham, trust God to raise up His solutions, answers, and blessings to bring Himself glory.

> **"(As it is written, I have made thee a father of many nations,) before him whom he believed, *even* God, who quickeneth (makes alive) the dead, and (God) calleth those things which be not as though they were." Romans 4:17**

God called forth Isaac out of Abraham's loins when it was an otherwise impossibility in the natural. In your life, beloved, **"Is there anything too hard for the LORD?"** (Gen. 18:14)

Our connection with God is all about relationship, and the quality of that relationship is exemplified in our prayer lives – or lack thereof. If a person is pursuing the LORD, he has a prayer life. He lays down his own desires and life and seeks God's life. This is perhaps in no other scrutiny seen more clearly than in the value he assigns to his prayer life, and the heart affections and time he is willing to invest in it.

In Psalms 63, the Psalmist captures the life of the person who truly has a heart after God.

> **"O God, thou *art* my God; early will I seek thee: my soul thirsteth for thee, my flesh longeth for thee in a dry and thirsty land, where no water is; To see thy power and thy glory, so *as* I have seen thee in the sanctuary. Because thy lovingkindness *is* better than life, my lips shall praise thee. Thus will I bless thee while I live: I will lift up my hands in thy name. My soul shall be satisfied as *with* marrow**

and fatness; and my mouth shall praise *thee* with joyful lips: When I remember thee upon my bed, *and* meditate on thee in the *night* watches. Because thou hast been my help, therefore in the shadow of thy wings will I rejoice. My soul followeth hard after thee: thy right hand upholdeth me." Psalms 63:1-8

The following is an excerpt from *My Utmost for His Highest*, by Oswald Chambers:

> "'At that day ye shall ask in My name.' John 16:26
>
> We are too much given to thinking of the Cross as something we have to get through; we get through it only in order to get into it. The Cross stands for one thing only for us - a complete and entire and absolute identification with the Lord Jesus Christ, and there is nothing in which this identification is realized more than in prayer.
>
> 'Your Father knoweth what things ye have need of, before ye ask Him.' Then why ask? The idea of prayer is not in order to get answers from God; prayer is perfect and complete oneness with God. If we pray because we want answers, we will get huffed with God. The answers come every time, but not always in the way we expect, and our spiritual huff shows a refusal to identify ourselves with Our Lord in prayer. We are not here to prove God answers prayer; we are here to be living monuments of God's grace.
>
> 'I say not that I will pray the Father for you: for the Father Himself loveth you.' Have you reached such an intimacy with God that the Lord Jesus Christ's life of prayer is the only explanation of your life of prayer? Has Our Lord's vicarious life become your

vital life? 'At that day' you will be so identified with Jesus that there will be no distinction.

When prayer seems to be unanswered, beware of trying to fix the blame on someone else. That is always a snare of Satan. You will find there is a reason which is a deep instruction to you, not to anyone else."

PRAYER: *Father, please bless me to honor You and Your will first and foremost in this life You have granted me, by my being authentically crucified with Christ. Please unite my heart to fear Your holy name and to number this short time on this earth as a gift from You. I love You, Jesus, and thank You for dying for my sins and for the resurrection power of the Holy Ghost You placed in me upon salvation, and the infilling of the Holy Spirit. You must increase and I must decrease. I declare and deliberately decide to place You first daily in my life – I am crucified with Christ. Early will I seek Thee. Amen.*

Capture Points

1. Discuss Psalms 5:3 along with Mark 1:35 and the importance of daily and first fruits prayer in the life of every disciple of Jesus.

2. Transcribe onto an index card and discuss Romans 12:1-2 (KJV recommended).

3. Write out on an index card Mark 10:27: **"And Jesus looking upon them saith, With men** *it is* **impossible, but not with God: for with God all things are possible."** (KJV)

Chapter Five

CONFESS THIS!
Declaring His Truth
Our Blessed Opportunity to Get Real with Jesus

"And they that are Christ's HAVE crucified the flesh with the affections and lusts." Galatians 5:24

Jesus said to get on the cross!

"And he said to them all, If any man will come after me, let him deny himself, and take up his cross daily, and follow me. For whosoever will save his life shall lose it: but whosoever will lose his life for my sake, the same shall save it." Luke 9:23-24

Do you believe that **"Death and life are in the power of the tongue"**? (Prov. 18:20-21)

What should we do to obey God concerning what He told us in this statement? Shall we use this verse to "exploit" Him – to use it as a tool to get things out of Him? Should we employ this truth for His glory or for our own benefit?

The apostle Paul said **"I die daily."** (1 Cor. 15:31)

Instead of confessing things that may further embellish our selfish, greedy, fruitless, covetous Laodicean lives, why not confess over and into our lives what the Bible tells us and from a disposition of humility and brokenness? Why not obey the LORD by confessing ourselves on the cross, where the self-serving must be nailed that His resurrection life might raise us up? Shall we profess with our lips He gave us that we are on the cross (crucified with Christ), instead of seeking to reign as kings over our own destinies, and rulers on the thrones of our own hearts?

The authentic disciple's prayerful confession of God's Word could go something like this (feel free to declare these as you read over them):

- I am crucified with Christ (Gal. 2:20).

- All my personal rights are hereby waived because I belong to Jesus and live only to bring Him glory (1 Cor. 1:29, 31).

- Without Jesus, I can do nothing of value in God's eyes (Jn. 15:5).

- Jesus can only work in and through me as my life is laid down – flattened in humility and totally dependent upon Him (Ps. 145:14; Jn. 15:5; Gal. 2:20).

- Father in Heaven, You promised it would happen to me, so I choose to embrace suffering, persecutions, ridicule, chastening, trials, tribulations, and mocking, for loving, declaring, and worshiping my LORD and Savior Jesus Christ (Matt. 10:22; 24:10-13; 2 Tim. 3:12; James 1:2-4).

- I am dead and my life is hid with Christ in God (Col. 3:3).

- As God blesses me to be used to communicate His truth and love, when I am persecuted, I will bless and pray for and love those who bring that persecution (Matt. 5:44; 2 Tim. 3:12).

- LORD Jesus, You must increase but I must decrease (Jn. 3:30).

- I am not my own but bought with the price of Christ's holy blood (1 Cor. 6:19-20).

- By the grace of God and Jesus' sacrifice, I am a new creature in Christ, and I now henceforth live to please Him and not myself (2 Cor. 5:15).

- Not my will but rather Thine be done, Father! (Lk. 22:42).

- Thank You, Father, for every breath and blessing You grant me in this life. Every good and every perfect gift comes from You (Heb. 13:1-6; James 1:18).

- I will beware and stay clear of covetousness because my significance is not based on what I possess materially or financially in this world (Lk. 12:15). I now choose to avoid and even openly expose any person in leadership who, through false teaching, feeds the lusts that Christ commanded to be crucified (Rom. 16:17-18; 2 Tim. 4:3-4).

- I abide this day thankful and content in knowing You, who are my exceeding great reward (Gen. 15:1; Phil. 4:11).

- I think it not strange concerning the fiery trials which are to try me for worshipping and serving You, Jesus. Such persecution and testing and trials clearly testify that the spirit of glory and of God rests upon my life by His grace (1 Pet. 4:12-14).

- As a follower of Jesus Christ, I choose to deny myself and not feed the depraved fleshly/sinful nature, and to rather glorify You, LORD, by doing Your will and not my own (Lk. 9:23-24).

- My body was made to glorify the LORD, who bought me with His own precious blood, and not to fornicate in any manner (1 Thess. 4:1-8).

- With the faculties You gave me, I choose to deliberately study, learn, meditate upon, and memorize Your Word, LORD, and live it out beginning this hour (Josh. 1:8; Prov. 4:4; Jn. 5:39; 2 Tim. 2:15; 3:16, 17).

- I choose to become learned in God's Word and to cease being a slothful and ignorant person, who does not understand the truths of the very God I claim to love (Ps. 119; 2 Tim. 2:15; 3:16-17).

- Heavenly Father, thank You for finding, saving, and blessing me to know You (Jer. 9:23-24; Jn. 17:3).

- Father in Heaven, thank You for blessing my life to be conformed to the image of Your Son, being made conformable to His death (Phil. 3:10).

- I praise You, LORD Jesus, for blessing me with Your fear and wisdom to not lean to my own understanding, but rather in all my thoughts and ways to acknowledge Your Word and the leading of Your Spirit in all things (Prov. 3:5-6).

- I love You, LORD Jesus. Please fill me with more of Your holy love (1 Thess. 4:9-10).

- This moment I denounce all self-idolatry and begin to worship You, LORD Jesus, in spirit and in truth! (Exod. 20:3-5; 1 Jn. 5:20-21)

- Realizing that the command of Jesus is to give up all or to lose out on all of His blessings, I turn fully to You, LORD. I this moment joyfully obey You, by releasing my whole being and existence (past, present and future) into Your infinite hands. I gladly release myself fully to You, the One who made me, and sent Your only begotten Son to be pierced for my sins and to earn my salvation (Lk. 14:33; 23:46; Acts 20:28).

- Joyfully and in utter gratitude, I give up all rights to my own life, that Christ might reign in and through this vessel (1 Cor. 6:19-20; 2 Cor. 4:7).

- I am a servant of Jesus Christ and He is my identity (Gal. 6:14; 1 Cor. 2:2).

- I will not allow any mere man, namely a leader, to take precedence over my worship, affection, obedience, and love for Jesus Christ, my nail-scarred risen Savior and LORD.

- In obedience to Jesus Christ my LORD and Savior, I choose to arise early and seek His face in prayer communion and Bible study, placing Him first place in my day (Ps. 5:3; 63:1, 8; Mk. 1:35).

- From this day forward, I choose to die to the self-life and to follow Christ by lifting up others above myself (Phil. 2:3-5).

- By God's enabling grace, I will obey the LORD by scheduling in times of fasting, prayer, and communion in seeking His holy face in earnest for His will to be accomplished in His body, Jerusalem, this nation, my family, the fellowship gatherings I am a part of, and my own life (Isa. 58).

- Moment by moment, I will commune with the truth/Word and allow it to direct my every thought and step in this life (Ps. 15:2; 19:14; 73:25; 119:105).

- In obedience to my LORD, I now begin to move into communicating the Gospel of Jesus, building up and praying for the saints of Christ, and discipling others by teaching them all things the LORD gave us in His Holy Word (Matt. 28:18-20; Col. 4:2, 12; Philemon 1:6-7).

- No more shall I be ashamed of the Gospel of Jesus Christ, in Jesus' precious name (Rom. 1:16).

- From this moment forward, I refuse to be one who claims to know Christ and yet doesn't know why I believe what I claim to believe. By His grace and my own will, I now move on toward perfection (maturity) by learning the elementary teachings of Christ and building upon that foundational knowledge (2 Tim. 2:15; Heb. 6:1-3).

"Death and life are in the power of the tongue." (Prov. 18:20-21) Instead of using this biblical truth/principle to gratify self by seeking to bring more fleeting material goods to benefit our own self-serving agendas, why not use it to humbly submit our lives genuinely under the mighty hand of God, in submission to the lordship of Christ Jesus? And this we should do, no matter what comes our way (1 Pet. 4:12-14).

Suffering is for our Good

Renegade rulers have been around since man has been on earth. The Bible is filled with such unjust rulers from Nimrod to the coming Antichrist. But the LORD uses hardships and injustices, brought about by unjust rulers, to bring about

His blessed character in our lives. Remember what God did during and after Joseph's sufferings?

> **"MANY are the afflictions of the righteous: but the LORD delivereth him out of them all." Psalms 34:19**

> **"Beloved, think it not strange concerning the fiery trial which is to try you, as though some strange thing happened unto you: But rejoice, inasmuch as ye are partakers of Christ's sufferings; that, when his glory shall be revealed, ye may be glad also with exceeding joy. If ye be reproached for the name of Christ, happy [are ye]; for the spirit of glory and of God resteth upon you: on their part he is evil spoken of, but on your part he is glorified." 1 Peter 4:12-14**

The LORD uses sufferings and delivers His people. While penning this book and simultaneously suffering personal hardships under the rule of an unjust earthly judge, this disciple was blessed to receive a personal exhortation from a dear brother in Christ. Here it is:

> "Brother, sink down into His wounds and hide yourself in His riven side, in the cleft of the Rock. Go down, get down into the dark and gloomy shade of His death where His wisdom, power, and riches are found (last half of Job 3 and chapter 28; Rom. 11:33). Waive your rights, give up control, suffer with Him. He will rise up in and around you and raise you and your circumstances from the dead. He will direct the heart of the judge. He will resurrect the fullness of your relationship with your son. He will open the grave and say, 'Todd, you and your son, come out!' Stand still, station yourself and see the glory of God. Love you, Bro. Travis"

This counsel was some of the most profound that this disciple has ever received. It went deep and rang true. It produced fruit and will continue to do so for the remainder of my days upon this earth.

Smiling Wolves who Teach a Suffer-Less False Gospel

Shallow people, who have chosen to serve self instead of the Savior, don't like to suffer; so they find wolves to tell them they don't have to (2 Tim. 4:3).

The ease-loving masses want a quick fix – they do not want to have to suffer, even though the Word tells us that those who believe are called **"also to suffer for his sake."** (Phil. 1:29) They want to be told that they don't have to suffer. Just like the false prophets of old, a myriad of beguilers have risen to the occasion to tell them just that (Isa. 30:9-10; 2 Tim. 4:2-4).

In reflecting upon the heretical Word-of-Faith teachers and teachings, I am reminded of what the Holy Ghost forewarned of in 2 Peter 2:

> **"But there were <u>false prophets</u> also among the people, even as <u>there shall be false teachers among you</u>, who privily (secretly) shall bring in damnable heresies (lies that damn the soul), even denying the Lord that bought them, and bring upon themselves swift destruction. And many shall follow their pernicious ways; by reason of whom the way of truth shall be evil spoken of. And through covetousness shall they with feigned words make merchandise of you: whose judgment now of a long time lingereth not, and their damnation slumbereth not." 2 Peter 2:1-3**

If we embrace divine truth, we will soon find ourselves seeking the LORD for ourselves and ridding our lives of the voices of evil wolves in leadership positions, even the slew of false teachers who have defied the LORD and led us astray via their false teaching. According to the biblical warning and revelation, false prophets lead people to worship at the altar of self, and are bringing judgment upon us and this nation (Isa. 5:24; 9:16; Rev. 2:14). The Word-of-Faith and mega church motivational teachers, who pose as godly pastors while trampling the Word of God, are monster deceivers in the eyes of a holy God. Their **"damnation slumbereth not."** (2 Pet. 2:1-3) That's right, the Word of the LORD tells us that these men are not just "nice, well-meaning, just misled men." No, look at what the Bible says about these leaders who are betraying the LORD by leading His precious flock into eternal perdition:

> **"His watchmen *are* blind: they are all ignorant, they are all dumb dogs, they cannot bark; sleeping, lying down, loving to slumber. Yea, they are greedy dogs *which* can never have enough, and they are shepherds that cannot understand: they all look to their own way, every one for his gain, from his quarter. Come ye, *say they*, I will fetch wine, and we will fill ourselves with strong drink (intoxicating doctrines); and tomorrow shall be as this day, and much more abundant (no judgment is coming is their attitude)." Isaiah 56:10-12**

> **"(For MANY *walk, of whom I have told you often, and now tell you even weeping, that they are* the <u>ENEMIES of the cross of Christ</u>: Whose end *is* destruction (hell), whose God is their belly (carnal appetites), and whose glory *is* in their shame, who mind earthly things.)" Philippians 3:18-19**

For more on this topic, read the following chapters which are intentionally divinely-inspired for the purpose of helping His saints identify and avoid wolves who wear sheep's clothing: Jeremiah 23; Ezekiel 34; Matthew 23; 2 Peter 2-3; Jude; Revelation 2-3. See book titled *Deceivers & False Prophets Among Us* at www.SafeGuardYourSoul.com.

It's time to cut off the false teachers of our day who have led us to believe that we are "little gods," and that by thinking and confessing all the right things we can order our own world, determine our own destinies, procure to ourselves whatever WE so desire, and do all of this without intimacy with Jesus Christ (Prov. 19:27). These beguilers have led millions to believe they can use God's Word against Him, and that He (the Almighty God) is forced or obligated to do whatever we confess by faith. This is witchcraft! Though they try to cleverly mask it, that's exactly what their diabolical theology boils down to.

Beware! These are deadly and toxic lies, beloved. Who in the world ever convinced believers that Jesus Christ came and died on a wooden cross so we could use His own words for our own selfish gain? Did Jesus tell us that He came to die for this? This message is the antichrist antithesis of the message of the Holy Bible and will end in ultimate destruction for those who are led astray by it. These men/women and their teachings lead people to build up what Jesus commanded to be crucified – sinful self. Jesus came to die in our place – for our sin – and called us to follow Him in laying down our lives in obedience to Him. Anyone who freely chooses not to obey His clear command to die to self does not know Him and will not be with Him eternally (Mk. 8:34-38; Lk. 9:23-24; 14:33).

> **"For ye are dead, and your life is hid with Christ in God." Colossians 3:3**

> **"For we are the circumcision, which worship God in the spirit, and rejoice in Christ Jesus, and have no confidence in the flesh." Philippians 3:3**

F.B. Meyer wrote:

> "Although Jesus was rich in all the divine fullness
> of His divine nature, He became poor and emptied
> Himself (see 2 Cor. 8:9). In other words, He
> determined not to speak His own words, follow His
> own scheme and plan, or work His mighty works in
> His own might. Rather, He became the channel and
> instrument through which His Father spoke, worked,
> and reconciled the world unto Himself. Let us, like
> Jesus, empty ourselves that we might be filled with
> God's mercy, power, and love." F.B. Meyer, *The Best
> of F.B. Meyer*, p. 180

God will raise up all those that be bowed down before His
Majesty in humility, depending upon Him for their every
breath, direction, empowerment, and inspiration.

> **"The LORD upholdeth all that fall, and raiseth up
> all those that be bowed down." Psalms 145:14**

When we are crucified with Christ experientially daily, we
will not speak our own words but rather those He would
lead us to speak.

> **"If thou turn away thy foot from the sabbath, from
> doing thy pleasure on my holy day (every day);
> and call the Sabbath (His rest) a delight, the holy
> of the LORD, honourable; and shalt honour him,
> not doing thine own ways, nor finding thine own
> pleasure, <u>nor speaking thine own words</u>." Isaiah
> 58:13**

The crucified life exemplifies Christ, who was granted **"the
tongue of the learned."**

> **<u>"The Lord GOD hath given me the tongue of the
> learned</u>, that I should know how to speak a word in
> season to him that is weary: he wakeneth morning**

by morning, he wakeneth mine ear to hear as the learned." Isaiah 50:4

"The heart of the wise teacheth his mouth, and addeth learning to his lips. Pleasant words are as an honeycomb, sweet to the soul, and health to the bones." Proverbs 16:23-24

PRAYER: *Father in Heaven, I announce my utter spiritual poverty and hopelessness without You! According to Your command, I approach Your sheer mercy through the shed blood of Jesus Christ, asking You to forgive me for serving myself instead of You, and even using Your own Word to justify such evil. I now denounce self-idolatry. Jesus, please cleanse me from such wickedness and wash away all my sins afresh. Please begin building Your true and eternal kingdom in my heart and life, and use me to help others in the same. Into Your hands, I now commend my spirit. I am not my own but rather bought by Your holy blood and surrendered to Your divine purpose for my life, as You gave me in Your Holy Word. Father, not my own will but Thine be done in this life You gave! I love You, Jesus! Amen.*

Capture Points

1. Write out on an index card and discuss Proverbs 18:20-21 (KJV recommended).

2. Read and discuss Isaiah 56:10-12 and 2 Peter 2:1-3.

3. On an index card, transcribe Colossians 3:3 - **"For ye are dead, and your life is hid with Christ in God."** (KJV)

Chapter Six

The Cross in Light of His Appearing

"And every man that hath this hope (of His return) in him purifieth himself, even as he is pure." 1 John 3:3

According to this important passage in 1 John, those who are looking for Him to soon return, live their lives in a chaste manner. If they do stumble, there is the swift act of repentance and mending their ways (Prov. 28:13). The person who is not fervently purifying His life of every thought, word, and deed that does not please his soon to return LORD, is not ready for the return of Christ, and his soul lies in jeopardy of damnation.

"Having therefore these promises, dearly beloved, let us cleanse ourselves from all filthiness of the flesh and spirit, perfecting holiness in the fear of God." 2 Corinthians 7:1

In light of both the personal responsibility He gave each of us and His soon return, Jesus sternly warned us of the very same temptations which are common to man:

> "Heaven and earth shall pass away: but my words shall not pass away. And take heed to yourselves, lest at any time your hearts be overcharged (weighed down) with surfeiting (overeating), and drunkenness, and cares of this life, and *so* that day come upon you unawares. For as a snare (trap) shall it come on all them that dwell on the face of the whole earth. Watch ye therefore, and pray always, that ye may be accounted worthy to escape all these things that shall come to pass, and to stand before the Son of man." Luke 21:33-36

Concerning these words of Jesus, Bill Wegener writes:

> "In Luke 21:34-36, if Jesus said pray that you will be counted worthy to escape the things that shall come upon the face of the earth, that can only mean that you might be counted unworthy if you don't pray. Who was he talking to? Ummm that is obvious, the Christians of course."

What solution did Jesus give us here? – **"Watch ye therefore, and pray always."** Make His house – your body – the place of prayer. As His temple of the Holy Ghost, make your vessel a sanctuary of worship, prayer, obedience, thanksgiving, and praise to Him (1 Cor. 3:16). Christ said:

> **"My house shall be called the house of prayer ..."**
> **Matthew 21:13**

Do we live our lives in prayerfulness? Are you praying **"without ceasing"?** (1 Thess. 5:17) Are we watching vigilantly as we wait upon and look for our LORD's soon return?

First, ask yourself if you truly believe He is coming. If you embrace this truth by faith, you will not faint.

"I had fainted, unless I had believed to see the goodness of the LORD in the land of the living. Wait on the LORD: be of good courage, and he shall strengthen thine heart: wait, I say, on the LORD." Psalms 27:13-14

"The goodness of the LORD" is coming to those who know and love Him, and the wrath of God is coming upon those who don't – **"he shall appear to your joy, and they shall be ashamed."** (Isa. 66:5)

According to our LORD, who is the **"resurrection and the life,"** there is going to be **"the resurrection of life"** and **"the resurrection of damnation."**

"Marvel not at this: for the hour is coming, in the which all that are in the graves shall hear his voice, And shall come forth; they that have done good, unto the resurrection of life; and they that have done evil, unto the resurrection of damnation." John 5:28-29

The heart cry of those who live expectantly looking for His soon return is as follows:

"He which testifieth these things saith, Surely I come quickly. Amen. Even so, come, Lord Jesus." Revelation 22:20

They **"have confidence"** as they look for His appearing:

"And now, little children, abide in him; that, when he shall appear, we may have confidence, and not be ashamed before him at his coming." 1 John 2:28

Today, instead of being **"poor in spirit,"** many who love self more than Jesus are proud, self-confident, self-reliant, and rich toward self rather than **"rich toward God."** (Lk. 12:21; 2 Tim. 3:1-7) They are emboldened toward the love of self by the world, but much more insidiously by those claiming to be representing Christ. The whole psychological movement that Satan began introducing wholesale into the church world in the 1960's and 1970's feeds the fleshly nature. It is the antithesis of Christ and His message to us to take up the cross and put to death the deeds of the body. This Luciferic rebellion is fostered, taught, and perpetuated through a myriad of conspiring deceivers, who fill pulpits and books with this evil lie that men can be as gods, and therefore all is to revolve around them (Gen. 3:5; Isa. 45:22; Ezek. 22:25, 27; 1 Tim. 2:5). Yet, in the divine economy, all revolves around Jesus Christ, *"who is* **the blessed and only Potentate, the King of kings, and Lord of lords."** (1 Tim. 6:15)

Those who choose to make themselves preeminent instead of Christ, are doomed to eternal destruction (Col. 1:18, 2:18-19; 2 Thess. 2:10-12). – **"They shall never see light."** (Ps. 49:19)

Christ alone will reign victorious, and those who know and obey Him to the end will reign with Him.

> **"And in the days of these kings shall the God of heaven set up a kingdom, which shall never be destroyed: and the kingdom shall not be left to other people,** *but* **it shall break in pieces and consume all these kingdoms, and it shall stand for ever ... I saw in the night visions, and, behold,** *one* **like the Son of man came with the clouds of heaven, and came to the Ancient of days, and they brought him near before him. And there was given him dominion, and glory, and a kingdom, that all people, nations, and languages, should serve him: his dominion** *is* **an everlasting dominion, which shall not pass away, and his kingdom** *that* **which shall not be destroyed ... But the saints of the most High shall take the**

> kingdom, and possess the kingdom for ever, even for ever and ever ... Until the Ancient of days came, and judgment was given to the saints of the most High; and the time came that the saints possessed the kingdom." Daniel 2:44; 7:13-14, 18, 22, 27

Fret not, beloved, antichrist must rise and come to world prominence before he can be utterly destroyed by Jesus Christ the Almighty (Rev. 1:8; 19:11-5). This must come to pass according to His prophetic utterances. As we await our conquering LORD and Messiah, let us be ever mindful of the potential in us to become antichrist ourselves by usurping His authority over our personal lives and reigning in His place (2 Tim. 3:5).

> "For of him, and through him, and to him, *are* all things: to whom *be* glory for ever. Amen." Romans 11:36

Jesus is coming - ready or not. He is going to soon appear to the blessing of some and the curse of many. Let's look at a beautiful passage from 2 Thessalonians 1:

> "So that we ourselves glory in you in the churches of God for your patience and faith in all your persecutions and tribulations that ye endure: *Which is* a manifest token of the righteous judgment of God, that ye may be counted worthy of the kingdom of God, for which ye also suffer: Seeing *it is* a righteous thing with God to recompense tribulation to them that trouble you; And to you who are troubled rest with us, when the Lord Jesus shall be revealed from heaven with his mighty angels, In flaming fire taking vengeance on them that know not God, and that obey not the gospel of our Lord Jesus Christ: Who shall be punished with everlasting destruction from the presence of

> the Lord, and from the glory of his power; When he shall come to be glorified in his saints, and to be admired in all them that believe (because our testimony among you was believed) in that day." 2 Thessalonians 1:4-10

"Your joy" will soon be full:

> **"Hear the word of the LORD, ye that tremble at his word; Your brethren that hated you, that cast you out for my name's sake, said, Let the LORD be glorified: <u>but he shall appear to your joy, and they shall be ashamed</u>." Isaiah 66:5**

Father, please keep us clothed in Your perfect righteousness!

> **"Behold, I come as a thief. Blessed *is* he that watcheth, and <u>keepeth his garments</u>, lest he walk naked, and they see his shame." Revelation 16:15**

The righteousness He gave us is to be kept by the recipient as he depends fully upon the glorious One, who bled to make him righteous (1 Cor. 6:19-20; 2 Cor. 5:15). In Scripture, the white robes of righteousness depict the righteousness of Christ given to His people, and spots in those garments represent sinfulness of the one who was at some past point made righteous and given that garment (2 Pet. 3:14; Jude 23; Rev. 4:4; 7:13; 16:15; 19:7-14). That garment is spotless when first given, and only sin allowed by the recipient can spot that garment. Those who are **"lukewarm"** are those who go back to sin without repenting, and whose garments are thereby spotted (Rev. 3:2-5; 14-21). Jesus beckons these backsliders to **"repent"** so that **"the shame of thy nakedness do not appear."** (Rev. 3:18-19)

To the church at Sardis, Jesus said:

> **"Be watchful, and strengthen the things which remain, that are ready to die: for I have not found**

thy works perfect before God. Remember therefore how thou hast received and heard, and hold fast, and repent. If therefore thou shalt not watch, I will come on thee as a thief, and thou shalt not know what hour I will come upon thee. <u>Thou hast a few names even in Sardis which have not defiled their garments; and they shall walk with me in white: for they are worthy.</u> He that overcometh, the same shall be clothed in white raiment; and I will not blot out his name out of the book of life, but I will confess his name before my Father, and before his angels." Revelation 3:2-5

In any group of Christians, some are keeping their garments white through walking in the light with Jesus, while others defile their garments by sinfulness. – **"Thou hast a few names even in Sardis which have not defiled their garments; and they shall walk with me in white: for they are worthy."** Speaking to the church in Sardis, Jesus said that there were only **"a few names ... which have not defiled their garments."** Only these, He continued, **"shall walk with me in white."**

Jesus said that the sins people commit are **"evil things"** and that they **"come from within."** This is why the cross is inward first and foremost. It affects the inner man and then shows up in the life. Christ told us that it is sin that **"defileth the man."** (Mk. 7:19-23)

"All these evil things come from within, and defile the man. And he said, That which cometh out of the man, that defileth the man. For from within, out of the heart of men, proceed evil thoughts, adulteries, fornications, murders, Thefts, covetousness, wickedness, deceit, lasciviousness, an evil eye, blasphemy, pride, foolishness: All these evil things

come from within, and defile the man." Mark 7:19-
23

In order to be in attendance at the Great Supper of the
Lamb, one must have on the wedding garment that only
Christ can give.

> "Go ye therefore into the highways, and as many as
> ye shall find, bid to the marriage. So those servants
> went out into the highways, and gathered together
> all as many as they found, both bad and good:
> and the wedding was furnished with guests. And
> when the king came in to see the guests, he saw
> there a man which had not on a wedding garment:
> And he saith unto him, <u>Friend, how camest thou in
> hither not having a wedding garment?</u> And he was
> speechless. Then said the king to the servants, Bind
> him hand and foot, and take him away, and cast
> *him* into outer darkness (one of the descriptions of
> hell); there shall be weeping and gnashing of teeth.
> For many are called, but few *are* chosen." Matthew
> 22:9-14

More on white robes:

> "After this I beheld, and, lo, a great multitude, which
> no man could number, of all nations, and kindreds,
> and people, and tongues, stood before the throne,
> and before the Lamb, clothed with white robes, and
> palms in their hands ... Saying, Amen: Blessing, and
> glory, and wisdom, and thanksgiving, and honour,
> and power, and might, *be* unto our God for ever
> and ever. Amen. And one of the elders answered,
> saying unto me, What are these which are arrayed
> in white robes? and whence came they? And I said
> unto him, Sir, thou knowest. And he said to me,
> These are they which came out of great tribulation,

and <u>have washed their robes, and made them white in the blood of the Lamb</u>." Revelation 7:9, 12-14

Those who keep their garments will **"die IN the Lord,"** as opposed to those who die OUTside the LORD. Only they who die abiding in Christ have the promise of eternal **"rest from their labours."**

> "Here is the patience (endurance) of the saints: here *are* they that keep the commandments of God, and the faith of Jesus. And I heard a voice from heaven saying unto me, Write, Blessed *are* the dead which die in the Lord from henceforth: Yea, saith the Spirit, that they may rest from their labours; and their works do follow them." Revelation 14:12-13

Those who are **"in the Lord"** are those who are preparing to meet Him. These are they who have been born again and are abiding in Christ – enduring to the end, loving Him with all that is in them.

> "And a voice came out of the throne, saying, Praise our God, all ye his servants, and ye that fear him, both small and great. And I heard as it were the voice of a great multitude, and as the voice of many waters, and as the voice of mighty thunderings, saying, Alleluia: for the Lord God omnipotent reigneth. Let us be glad and rejoice, and give honour to him: for the marriage of the Lamb is come, and <u>his wife hath made herself ready</u>. And to her was granted that she should be arrayed in fine linen, clean and white: for the fine linen is the righteousness of saints. And he saith unto me, Write, Blessed *are* they which are called unto the marriage supper of the Lamb. And he saith unto me, These are the true sayings of God." Revelation 19:5-9

Here's more on personal holiness in light of Christ's soon appearing:

> "But the day of the Lord will come as a thief in the night; in the which the heavens shall pass away with a great noise, and the elements shall melt with fervent heat, the earth also and the works that are therein shall be burned up. *Seeing* then *that* all these things shall be dissolved, what manner *of persons* ought ye to be in *all* holy conversation and godliness, <u>Looking for and hasting unto the coming of the day of God</u>, wherein the heavens being on fire shall be dissolved, and the elements shall melt with fervent heat? Nevertheless we, according to his promise, look for new heavens and a new earth, wherein dwelleth righteousness. Wherefore, beloved, seeing that ye look for such things, be diligent that ye may be found of him in peace, without spot, and blameless." 2 Peter 3:10-14

The notion that we are unconditionally eternally secure is utterly foreign to Scripture. One simply must participate with the Savior by dying to the sinful self. How can we possibly claim to know the LORD and yet not cooperate with Him by obeying His righteous commands? Christ asks:

> "And why call ye me, Lord, Lord, and do not the things which I say?" Luke 6:46

One must **"die daily"** to remain in the state of readiness to meet the LORD – whether by His return or one's mortal demise. We cannot be raised up if we are not buried with Him in his death (Rom. 6).

Is not baptism a picture of death, burial, and resurrection? Let us observe what the apostle, under the direct inspiration of the Holy Ghost, penned in Colossians 2:

"In whom also ye are circumcised with the circumcision made without hands, in putting off the body of the sins of the flesh by the circumcision of Christ: Buried with him in baptism, wherein also ye are risen with him through the faith of the operation of God, who hath raised him from the dead." Colossians 2:11-12

As given us clearly by our LORD and His apostles, suffering the death of the flesh is part and parcel of New Testament living (Lk. 9:23-24; Rom. 6; Col. 3:3; 1 Pet. 2:21; 4:1). Remember that we are here to **"know him"** and be **"made conformable to his death,"** that we might experience ongoing fellowship with Him who is holy (Rom. 829; Phil. 3:10). This requires being made one with Him.

In our lives, there is that ever-present sin crouching at the door (Gen. 4:7). It is in our hearts – the sin nature in us is evil and **"desperately wicked,"** craving that which displeases our LORD who is **"holy, holy, holy."** (Gen. 6:5; Isa. 6:3; Jer. 17:9; Rom. 7:18, 24; Rev. 4:8) By divine decree, the old man must be sentenced to death by all who will reign with Him (2 Cor. 1:9; Gal. 2:20; 5:24; 6:14). The self and sin-serving nature must be crucified. If not, what would be the reason we are instructed to **"die daily"**? What would be the need to be **"crucified with Christ"**? (Gal. 2:20)

According to Christ, only a few will be ready when He returns. In light of His return, He instructed those who would be ready and escape those things which will shortly come to pass, to:

"And take heed to yourselves, lest at any time your hearts be overcharged (weighed down) with surfeiting (overeating), and drunkenness, and cares of this life, and *so* that day come upon you unawares. For as a snare (trap) shall it come on

all them that dwell on the face of the whole earth. Watch ye therefore, and pray always, that ye may be accounted worthy to escape all these things that shall come to pass, and to stand before the Son of man." Luke 21:34-36

Jesus warns that in order to live in His presence, overcoming anything that could defile the clean garments He issued to us, the disciple must:

"Watch and pray, that ye enter not into temptation: the spirit indeed is willing, but the flesh is weak." Matthew 26:41

PRAYER: *Father, please accept my sincere repentance in thinking and espousing my own thoughts in lieu of Thy Holy Word. Your thoughts are high above mine and supremely superior. I this moment repent of my rebellion against You. Bless and quicken my spirit in Thy holy fear. Slay every idol of my heart so that You alone might reign as King in my heart! By Your grace and Spirit and my own will, I am crucified with Christ. I now beg You to set me apart for Your eternal glory, my LORD and God. Amen.*

Capture Points

1. Discuss 1 John 3:3 and the surrounding verses, and how this truth should be applied in the daily life of the disciple (1 Jn. 2:24-3:3).

2. Read and discuss the words of our LORD Jesus as recorded in Luke 21:33-36.

3. Write out Revelation 16:15 on and index card so that you can meditate upon and memorize it: **"Behold, I come as a thief. Blessed *is* he that watcheth, and <u>keepeth his garments,</u> lest he walk naked, and they see his shame."** (KJV)

Chapter Seven

"O Wretched Man that I Am!"
Romans 7:24

"O wretched man that I am! who shall deliver me from the body of this death?" Romans 7:24

Here's some interesting commentary on Romans from the *Believer's Bible Commentary:*

"Romans 7:23 But he sees a contrary principle at work in his life, striving against the new nature, and making him a captive of indwelling sin; George Cutting writes:

> 'The law, though he delights in it after the inward man, gives him no power. In other words, he is trying to accomplish what God has declared to be an utter impossibility—namely, making the flesh subject to God's holy law. He finds that the flesh minds the things of the flesh, and is very enmity itself to the law of God, and even to God Himself.' George Cutting, *The Old Nature and the New Birth*

Romans 7:24 Now Paul lets out his famous, eloquent groan. He feels as if he has a decomposing body strapped to his back. That body, of course, is the old nature in all its corruption. In his wretchedness he acknowledges that he is unable to deliver himself from this offensive, repulsive bondage. He must have help from some outside source." William MacDonald, *Believer's Bible Commentary*, p. 1707, 1708

Though we have been made the righteousness of God in Christ, we still retain the sinful nature, in which lies the ever crouching potential and tendency toward sin (Rom. 6-7; 2 Cor. 5:21). There is complete victory in Christ's grace (Rom. 6:14).

"This I say then, <u>Walk in the Spirit, and ye shall not fulfil the lust of the flesh. For the flesh lusteth against the Spirit, and the Spirit against the flesh: and these are contrary the one to the other</u>: so that ye cannot do the things that ye would." Galatians 5:16-17**

Notice closely here this segment of Holy Writ – **"the flesh lusteth against the Spirit, and the Spirit against the flesh."** By the Holy Spirit, Paul is showing the war that is raging in our members to see who will rule. The flesh is relentless. It is insoluble and unsolvable. The fleshly nature will not be completely conquered till death and departure from **"the body of this death."** (Rom. 7:24) Such a war is common to all men born after Adam. The Adamic or sinful nature is contrary to the Holy Spirit and will of God – **"Because the carnal mind *is* enmity against God: for it is not subject to the law of God, neither indeed can be."** (Rom. 8:7)

That which is not subject to God's holy and just standard – His law – is at enmity with Him. The sinful nature is the hostile enemy of a holy God. It must be therefore subdued by a life of crucifixion, and the enabling and overcoming power of the grace of the Holy Spirit of God dominating that life.

Of this truth, Andrew Murray wrote:

> "What the Holy Spirit does is to give the victory. 'If ye through the Spirit do mortify the deeds of the flesh, ye shall live.' It is the Holy Ghost who does this—the third Person of the Godhead. He it is who, when the heart is opened wide to receive Him, comes in and reigns there, and mortifies the deeds of the body, day by day, hour by hour, and moment by moment." *Absolute Surrender*

It is only through the working of the grace of God in Christ, by the power of the Holy Spirit and our faith, that the righteous standards of the LORD can be fulfilled. Regenerate man is made new – **"all things are of God"** – and he can be filled and led, empowered, and propelled by the very divine Person of the Holy Ghost (2 Cor. 5:18).

"Do we then make void the law through faith? God forbid: yea, we establish the law." Romans 3:31

"For the law of the Spirit of life in Christ Jesus hath made me free from the law of sin and death ... That the righteousness of the law might be fulfilled in us, who walk not after the flesh, but after the Spirit." Romans 8:2, 4

It's only through **"the law of the Spirit of life in Christ Jesus"** that one can be made and kept **"free from the law of sin and death."** (Rom. 8:2) This book and all books of the Bible are written to God's people and not the lost. According to this very passage, those who walk in the fleshly lusts (live in sin) are under the **"condemnation"** of the LORD (Rom. 8:1). Spiritual death is the end result that comes to all who "live after the flesh." (Rom. 8:13) "Be not deceived; God is not mocked: for whatsoever a man soweth, that shall he also reap. For he that soweth to his flesh shall of the flesh reap corruption; but he that soweth to the Spirit shall of the Spirit reap life everlasting." (Gal. 6:7-8)

There is only one way to prevent becoming a "castaway," and that is to "keep under" the sinful nature – to sentence it to death (1 Cor. 9:27; 2 Cor. 1:9).

> "For they that are after the flesh do mind the things of the flesh; but they that are after the Spirit the things of the Spirit. For <u>to be carnally minded is death;</u> but to be spiritually minded is life and peace. Because the carnal mind is enmity against God: for it is not subject to the law of God, neither indeed can be. So then they that are in the flesh cannot please God." Romans 8:5-8

Concerning this, L. E. Maxwell wrote:

> "To the flesh, the Cross is God's verdict. God's 'sentence of death.' Paul traveled a long road to learn 'that in me (that is, in my flesh,) dwelleth no good thing.'
>
> 'Is it indeed to me,' cries the awakened believer, 'that these very things apply?' It does seem to take a long time to learn that the mind of the flesh 'is enmity against God.' It is therefore 'not subject to the law of God, neither indeed can be' (Romans 8:7). The verdict has gone forth, the sentence executed. The only cure is condemnation, crucifixion, death with Christ. The flesh with all its foul brood has been put to the hanged man's doom. To the accursed tree, Christ nailed 'the flesh with its affections and lusts.' There Christ reversed all the processes of nature; the old life was terminated to make room for the new,

for death can never inherit life. And 'to be carnally minded is death.' The flesh has about it the smell of infernal associations. It stinks. Since its mind is already death, God sent it to its own place – the cross." L. E. Maxwell, *Embraced by the Cross*, p. 88

"For I know that in me (that is, in my flesh,) dwelleth no good thing: for to will is present with me; but how to perform that which is good I find not." Romans 7:18

The sin nature is ever present, crouched, and ready for the slightest opportunity to lunge out like a venomous snake at its unsuspecting victim. In fact, we are all born in sin and therefore have no hope of pleasing God outside of the intervening of the LORD Himself, and no man can come to Him unless the Father draws him (Jn. 6:44).

"Wherefore, as by one man (Adam) sin entered into the world, and death by sin; and so <u>death passed upon all men</u>, for that all have sinned." Romans 5:12

Of this passing or descent from life to death by sin, John D. Morris, Ph.D. writes:

"The Bible plainly teaches that 'the wages of sin is death' (Romans 6:23). Before Adam and Eve rebelled, animals ate only plants (Genesis 1:30). Death came as a result of sin and the curse: 'For in the day that thou eatest thereof the forbidden tree thou shalt surely die' (Genesis 2:17). The first death in all of creation occurred when God provided Adam and Eve animal skins for clothing. Sin always brings death. 'By one man sin entered into the world, and death by sin; and so death passed upon all men, for that all have sinned' (Romans 5:12). Indeed 'the whole creation groaneth and travaileth in pain together until now'

95

(Romans 8:22). That this is not referring to spiritual death only is clear from our text, which deals with physical resurrection from the dead. Just as Adam's sin brought death on all creation, so Christ's resurrection brings victory over death." (This article was originally published October, 2001. *Death Before Sin?*, Institute for Creation Research, http://www.icr.org/article/18303/)

Speaking of and contrasting between the two Adams – the fall of the first and the resurrection of the second – the Scripture tells us:

> **"For since by man (Adam) came death, by man (Jesus) came also the resurrection of the dead. For as in Adam all die, even so in Christ shall all be made alive." I Corinthians 15:21, 22**

When man sinned, there was incurred a spiritual death or separation from his Maker. Shortly after the fall of man into sin and death, when Cain had chosen to do things his own way instead of God's, the LORD had this to say to him:

> **"And the LORD said unto Cain, Why art thou wroth (mad)? and why is thy countenance fallen? If thou doest well, shalt thou not be accepted? and if thou doest not well, sin lieth at the door ... " Genesis 4:6-7**

Every man has a choice. God gives all men choice in this life. We see this with God's dealings with Cain here – **"IF thou doest well, shalt thou not be accepted? and IF thou doest not well, sin lieth at the door."** Regrettably, in the case of Cain, he chose to do things his own way instead of God's way. He will forever dwell in the punishment of fire.

Since the sin of the first man and woman, spiritual **"death"** has **"passed upon upon all men"** born after them, and it is not until the redemption of the body that sin will be vanquished (Rom. 5:12; 1 Cor. 15:26).

> **"And if children, then heirs; heirs of God, and joint-heirs with Christ; if so be that we suffer with him, that we may be also glorified together. For I reckon that the sufferings of this present time are not worthy to be compared with the glory which shall be revealed in us. For the earnest expectation of the creature waiteth for the manifestation of the sons of God. For the creature was made subject to vanity, not willingly, but by reason of him who hath subjected the same in hope, Because the creature itself also shall be delivered from the bondage of corruption into the glorious liberty of the children of God. For we know that the whole creation groaneth and travaileth in pain together until now. And not only they, but ourselves also, which have the firstfruits of the Spirit, even we ourselves groan within ourselves, waiting for the adoption, to wit, the redemption of our body." Romans 8:17-23**

The saint must suffer with Christ, the sinless One. He must suffer the death of the self-life or life of sin. It's only those who suffer in their flesh who will be freed from sin's dominion by the blessed grace of the LORD (Rom. 6:7, 14). To **"know Him,"** the Heaven-bound believer must join the Son of God in **"the fellowship of his sufferings, being made conformable unto his death."** (Phil. 3:10) The very divinely-stated purpose for the redemption of mankind is that we would be **"conformed to the image of his Son."** (Rom. 8:29)

Remember the apostle Paul's big question in the heat of toiling and contending with his own unrelenting sinful nature? – **"O wretched man that I am! who shall deliver me from the body of this death?"** (Rom. 7:24) The answer to this all-important question is *God*. Only the LORD, who made man, can redeem him. He is the only One capable of accomplishing this; the Father sent His only begotten Son. His creation has been wayward since sin entered the world, and as we read in Romans 8 above, He alone can redeem it. The LORD delivers the born again saint now with overcoming divine grace, and will ultimately deliver us from all sin and even the subjection to its temptation. The enduring Christian, saved by His grace, must willingly suffer the death of his own will and sinful nature – **"IF so be that we suffer with him, that we may be also glorified together."** (Rom. 8:17) Did you catch that condition? Some teach and would like to think that since we are saved by His grace, the believer has no personal responsibility, but this is nonsense and not biblical. The repeated **"if"'s** of Holy Scripture denote condition and upend such a fallacy that seeks to turn **"the grace of God into lasciviousness,"** which is a license for sin (Jude 3-4).

Do you know what the Bible tells us is the **"last enemy"** that shall be conquered?

> **"For he must reign, till he hath put all enemies under his feet. The last enemy that shall be destroyed is death." 1 Corinthians 15:25-26**

Even the temptation to sin will be removed when we are with the LORD, in His very presence. The curse will be completely removed when Christ reigns on earth (Isa. 11:6; Rev. 21-22). But for now there is a test – a probationary period. Those who are born again must abide (remain) in Christ and thereby overcome sin, in order to be in and with Him (Matt. 10:22; Col. 1:23; Heb. 3:12-15; 10:26-39; 1 Pet. 1:9; 2 Pet. 2:20-22; Rev. 2-3). We must remain dead in Christ and buried with Him, that His resurrection power might reign in us and disable sin (Rom. 6). God is **"holy, holy, holy,"** yet most theology today is completely void of this utterly cardinal doctrine of the divine nature (Isa. 6:3; Rev. 4:8). It erroneously supposes that because He saved us, the immutable God now somehow lost His divine attribute of holiness, and now indiscriminately overlooks the sin of His people. Nothing could be more wrong (2 Cor. 7:1, 9-10; 1 Jn. 1:9). The once saved person living in sin is not secure. He is in trouble, regardless of any previous spiritual state he may have experienced with the LORD (Ezek. 33:12-13; Heb. 3:12-15; 10:26-39; 2 Pet. 2:20-22). God will punish sin. He is still holy and the wages of sin is still death (Gen. 2:17; Ezek. 18:4; Rom. 6:23; Rev. 21:8, 27).

Here is a glimpse of the glorious liberty the children of God have to look forward to:

> **"For our conversation is in heaven; from whence also we look for the Saviour, the Lord Jesus Christ: Who shall change our vile body, that it may be fashioned like unto his glorious body, according to the working whereby he is able even to subdue all things unto himself." Philippians 3:20-21**

All who enter His heavenly gates will receive a new body that is void of sin and immune from being tempted to sin. As we spoke of previously, it is only the LORD Almighty who can subdue the curse on creation which came by man's sin – **"according to the working whereby he is able even to subdue all things unto himself."** Jesus is the curse's only Cure.

The sin nature resides within all men after the fall (Rom. 5:12). Our LORD made it clear that the only way to overcome is to **"watch and pray."** (Matt. 26:41) **"Sin lieth at the door;"** it is there – in us, ever crouching like a prowling tiger, ready to strike as soon as there is an opening. Any person who is not born again and currently choosing to be heavenly minded in the power of the Spirit, is going to be dominated by sin. Jesus died to redeem us – to bring us into relationship with the Father and grant power over sin. Only God can overcome our sin, and He only does that as we delight in and obey Him. Sin is ready to attack, and if we but refuse to seek God the way He has prescribed, we shall be dominated by sin and death, for **"the wages of sin is death."** (Rom. 6:23) The inherent sin nature, or Adamic nature, rules every life until a greater power distills and overcomes it.

> **"For the law of the Spirit of life in Christ Jesus hath made me free from the law of sin and death." Romans 8:2**

"I am carnal, sold under sin," and yet the eclipsing power of divine grace through Jesus Christ is the glorious victory given to the saints of the Most High (Rom. 7:14; 1 Cor. 15:57). Grace overpowers sin in the lives of all who are truly and fully submitted to Christ (Rom. 6:14; James 4:7). Every human life that does not possess the eclipsing power and grace of Jesus Christ, is dominated by sin. This resurrection grace procures to us that victory as we experience what Paul termed as **"Always bearing about in the body the dying of the Lord Jesus."** (2 Cor. 4:10) When we are **"Always (perpetually) bearing about in the body the dying of the Lord Jesus,"** His blessed divine life will always or perpetually be manifesting in our mortal bodies, as death is working in us, and life through us to others (2 Cor. 4:10-12). Any person who is walking in and led by the Holy Spirit of God is dying downward and being simultaneously lifted upward by the resurrecting power of the Most High. He is therefore fruitful and blessed, and his leaf shall not wither, but be ever fruitful to God's glory (Ps. 1:3).

The unsaved or carnal man, religious though he may be, finds nothing in him to sacrifice to Christ and His work. In contrast, the person who is fully given over to Christ is truly saved, and therefore finds ways to be a blessing. He is dead to self, and Christ's life in him has swallowed up the self-life. He has ceased being given over to finding ways to spend more time and money on further embellishing his own life, but rather finds opportunities to bless others and to further the work of the Gospel. In this he lays up treasure in Heaven, and because of his obedience to Christ, his heart affections follow his giving into heavenly places (Matt. 6:19-21; Lk. 16:9-10).

It is when we are conformed to His death to sin and self-will, **"that the life also of Jesus"** is **"made manifest in our body."** (2 Cor. 4:10-11) It is as **"death"** works in us that Christ's **"life"** works out from us into the lives of others (2 Cor. 4:12).

> "It is into His *death* that we are to be rooted. We cannot ever pass on into a life where we get past the cross, or advance to any goal, leaving the cross behind. To do so is like a tree refusing to root itself into the ground. We are to reckon ourselves 'dead indeed unto sin' living unto God, but it is 'IN CHRIST JESUS.' 'In Him' we must be 'rooted,' and 'in Him' have our 'foundation,' whereon we are continually to be built up; i.e., we must ever be *striking our roots deeper into His death.*" Jessie Penn-Lewis, *The Centrality of the Cross*, p. 63

It is in being rooted down into His death, buried with Him, that **"sin that dwelleth in"** us is disallowed to carry out its evil and defiling **"motions."** (Rom. 7:5, 17, 20) It is in being rooted deeply into His death that we are assured of His raising power.

> **"Knowing that he which raised up the Lord Jesus shall raise up us also by Jesus, and shall present us with you." 2 Corinthians 4:14**

This revolutionary, divine work in the lives He redeems – **"the operation of God,"** this Gospel working, all begins at the new birth, when one is drawn in by the Father, is brought to full repentance, is fallen down prostrate upon the mercy of Jesus Christ, and is regenerated by the Holy Ghost (Jn. 3:1-8; Col. 2:12; Tit. 3:5-7).

Christ's **"life"** conquers all **"death."** Spiritual **"death"** cannot coexist with the divine life of Jesus working in the life of the submitted saint.

Paul told us that the law of God is **"holy, and the commandment holy, and just, and good"** and that it is **"spiritual: but I am carnal, sold under sin."** (Rom. 7:12-14)   There is nothing wrong with the law of God – it is perfect, but we are not. Fallen man is the problem, not the perfect divine law. Though redeemed, we have inherited a sinful nature from Adam (Rom. 5:12). Such a nature cannot be ousted, which would seem far easier than having to contend with it daily.

> **"But if the Spirit of him that raised up Jesus from the dead dwell in you, he that raised up Christ from the dead shall also quicken your mortal bodies by his Spirit that dwelleth in you. Therefore, brethren, we are debtors, not to the flesh, to live after the flesh. For if ye live after the flesh, ye shall die: but if ye through the Spirit do mortify the deeds of the body, ye shall live. For as many as are led by the Spirit of God, they are the sons of God."** Romans 8:11-14

Though victory comes to those who live in the Spirit by His grace, we are prone to sin whenever our carnal nature is given that opportunity – not kept under/subdued. Pay close attention to the divinely-inspired words of Paul the apostle in Romans 7:

"For we know that the law is spiritual: but I am carnal, sold under sin. For that which I do I allow not: for what I would, that do I not; but what I hate, that do I. If then I do that which I would not, I consent unto the law that *it is* good. Now then it is no more I that do it, but sin that dwelleth in me. For I know that in me (that is, in my flesh,) dwelleth no good thing: for to will is present with me; but *how* to perform that which is good I find not. For the good that I would I do not: but the evil which I would not, that I do. Now if I do that I would not, it is no more I that do it, but sin that dwelleth in me. I find then a law, that, when I would do good, evil is present with me. For I delight in the law of God after the inward man: But I see another law in my members, warring against the law of my mind, and bringing me into captivity to the law of sin which is in my members. O wretched man that I am! who shall deliver me from the body of this death? I thank God through Jesus Christ our Lord. So then with the mind I myself serve the law of God; but with the flesh the law of sin." Romans 7:14-25

Paul here tells us that he attempted to keep the law, which is holy and spiritual, and therein failed due to being **"sold under sin."** (Rom. 7:14) The holy law magnified his sinfulness and revealed how that **"no good thing"** dwelled in his flesh (Rom. 7:18). He said that **"evil is present"** in him and all of us after Adam's sin. We are all **"sold under sin,"** and it is only Jesus Christ that can deliver us from sin which brings death – separation from God (Rom. 7:14).

Paul the apostle wasn't saying he actually did those sins, but that sin was present in his nature and that there was **"no good thing"** in him, that is, in his flesh (Rom. 7:18).

Here in Romans 7 beginning in verse 14, Paul is speaking of the wretchedness of the sin-prone heart outside of being redeemed and presently captured in the grace of God. Yes, we have been made new creatures in Christ, and yet we must **"die daily"** to that carnal man which is **"sold under sin"** in order for Christ's new nature to prevail (Rom. 7:14; 1 Cor. 9:27). The LORD gave us a **"new heart"** upon regenerating and saving us, and it is in fully yielding to Him that we are pleasing to Him (Ezek. 36:26; Rom. 12:1). Such surrender includes crucifying that contrary sinful nature through the Holy Spirit's power (Rom. 8:13-14).

In Romans 6:12, we are instructed to **"Let not sin therefore reign in your mortal body, that ye should obey it in the lusts thereof."** He then says, **"Neither yield ye your members *as* instruments of unrighteousness unto sin: but yield yourselves unto God, as those that are alive from the dead, and your members *as* instruments of righteousness unto God."** (Rom. 6:13)

> **"For this is the love of God, that we keep his commandments: and his commandments are not grievous. For whatsoever is born of God overcometh the world: and this is the victory that overcometh the world, *even* our faith. Who is he that overcometh the world, but he that believeth that Jesus is the Son of God?" 1 John 5:3-5**

Many seek to conquer cities and nations, who have not conquered their own carnal nature.

> **"*He that is* slow to anger *is* better than the mighty; and he that ruleth his spirit than he that taketh a city." Proverbs 16:32**

> **"He that *hath* no rule over his own spirit *is like* a city *that is* broken down, *and* without walls." Proverbs 25:28**

"Temperance" is one dimension of the fruit produced by the Holy Spirit in the life of every true abiding Christian (Gal. 5:22-23). There is the ever-present war to be won over the self-life, and it is only by the power of the Holy Ghost that there can ever be hope to accomplish such. Jesus told us that we would receive power after that the Holy Ghost is come upon us. He is the Comforter Christ has sent forth to dwell in and with us, and He works in juxtaposition with the willing and obedient child of God to bring forth fruit and victory (Isa. 1:19-20). He will not force, but requires that the individual heart affections be engaged in obedient faith. He desires our victory more than can be imagined, and yet does not hand out victory to the one who will not yield.

Paul spoke of **"sin that dwelleth in me,"** and since God is holy, such sin must not be lived in or it will contaminate and sever the relationship (Rom. 7:17, 20; 2 Cor. 6:14-7:1; 1 Pet. 1:15-16). Forgiveness and divine, enabling grace await a bold approach to the throne of grace in honest repentance (Heb. 4:16; 1 Jn. 1:9).

> **"For godly sorrow worketh repentance to salvation (deliverance; victory) ... " 2 Corinthians 7:10**

This is a war in our inner man. It's a war that reveals who we love most – Jesus or self. The Son of God said that **"No man can serve two masters: for either he will hate the one, and love the other; or else he will hold to the one, and despise the other ..."** (Matt. 6:24)

This **"form of doctrine"** which is **"delivered you"** in the Holy Scriptures, defies the diabolical lie that once a person is brought by the LORD into His kingdom, that person can never forfeit his place in that eternal kingdom. Being saved is volitional, and so is continuing to walk with and in Christ (Deut. 30:19; Isa. 1:19-20; Jn. 15:1-6; Rom. 6:16; 11:19-22; Heb.

3:6, 12-15; 10:26-39; Rev. 2-3). Not one verse of Scripture, taken within its biblical context, automatically guarantees eternal security without condition. According to the very One who is our salvation, eternal security is only for those who currently hear His voice and are following Him (Jn. 10:27-29). Only those who **"abide"** or remain in Jesus after being saved, will taste of the eternal blessings of that **"new Jerusalem, which cometh down out of heaven."**

> **"Because thou hast kept the word of my patience, I also will keep thee from the hour of temptation, which shall come upon all the world, to try them that dwell upon the earth. Behold, I come quickly: hold that fast which thou hast, that no man take thy crown. Him that overcometh will I make a pillar in the temple of my God, and he shall go no more out: and I will write upon him the name of my God, and the name of the city of my God,** *which is* **new Jerusalem, which cometh down out of heaven from my God: and** *I will write upon him* **my new name."**
> **Revelation 3:10-12**

Note closely here that first of all, Jesus tells us that He will only eternally save and keep for Himself those who keep the word of His patience. In other words, He will keep those who endure with and abide/remain in Him. This condition, concept, and testimony is consistent throughout God's Word. Then He tells us that He is coming **"quickly,"** and instructs us to **"hold that fast which thou hast, that no man take thy crown."** If no man could take or cause us to forfeit our crown, why would Christ have bothered to warn us of such? Is Jesus Christ a lunatic, or is there real danger in allowing ourselves to be deceived and misled by men? (Col. 2:8; 2 Pet. 3:17) No such warning, of which there are many in Scripture, would appear if such weren't possible.

Are you beginning to see why dying to self **"daily"** is so vitally important? How can I possibly remain true to Jesus and my own self-interests simultaneously? Impossible! – **"No man can serve two masters."** (Matt. 6:24)

Loving the LORD is a command from God and yet it is a choice – **"Choose ye this day whom ye will serve."** (Josh. 24:15)

> **"What then? shall we sin, because we are not under the law, but under grace? God forbid. <u>Know ye not, that to whom ye yield yourselves servants to obey, his servants ye are to whom ye obey; whether of sin unto death, or of obedience unto righteousness?</u> But God be thanked, that ye were the servants of sin, but ye have obeyed from the heart that form of doctrine which was delivered you."** Romans 6:15-17

The life of self is death – the death of self is life.

"He must increase, but I must decrease." John 3:30

The way of the cross is the harder way, especially at first. Once the blessed resurrection life begins to raise that laid down life upward into rich fruit-bearing seasons, there is great rejoicing and plentiful reward. The presence and rush of His divine life in us can become enthralling, causing in our hearts a greater desire to sink down deeper into His death and burial (Rom. 6:3-4).

The counterfeit Christian takes the easy way out. He is drawn to those authors and speakers who, while holding positions of influence, are more like New Age motivational speakers who are selling people on the idea of making self better. The self-life is already condemned by God – there is no good thing that dwells in our flesh (Rom. 6-8). **"All"** of our **"righteousnesses"** are as **"filthy rags"** in the sight of a God who is **"holy, holy, holy."** (Isa. 6:3; 64:6; Rev. 4:8). Jesus told us to **"deny"** self and not try to build on its futile foundation (Ps. 39:5; Lk. 9:23-24). These well-funded beguilers cherry pick Scripture that they can assimilate into their self-indulgent, self-love "success" messages, and are leading people down the wide road that leads to destruction (Prov. 14:12; Matt. 7:13-14; 2 Pet. 2:1-3). It is only through the cross and the desert that true victory and success in the promised land of the LORD's blessings can be experienced (Deut. 8; Jn. 12:24-25). It is only in losing one's life that he can gain it back in a state that pleases the Creator, and keep it eternally (Matt. 16:24-26). This is the message of Holy Writ, and any message that varies is apostate (Isa. 8:20).

The key to realize is that we can't get to the resurrection until we first lay down and die, surrendering all to our LORD God and Savior.

The fleshly, sinful nature will not and does not go away unless it is put down by sentencing it to death.

Be sure that in you there is no intention to justify sin whatsoever (Rom. 6:1-2; Tit. 2:11-12). There is certainly a war raging in our members. **"I die daily"** – the flesh must be overcome daily and cannot be cast out. It must be daily crucified. While we have been given freedom from the law, if we go back under the law by sinning, then we are not under the enabling grace of God, which is the only way one can be saved (Rom. 6:1-2, 15; Heb. 10:26-39).

It takes more to overcome the flesh than renewing the mind, and even knowing and planting the seed of the Word. The whole life must be laid down – offered as a living sacrifice to the LORD. In that He so wonderfully and thoroughly bought us back to Himself, this is our **"reasonable service."** (Rom. 12:1-2)

Jesus said we must **"watch and pray that ye enter not into temptation."** (Matt. 26:41) Those who don't pray effectively – as He prescribed – will of a certainty enter into temptation. Part of praying is laying down our lives. The suffering He endured on the cross drove our LORD to cry out in desperation to the Father – **"And when Jesus had cried with a loud voice, he said, Father, into thy hands I commend my spirit: and having said thus, he gave up the ghost."** (Lk. 23:46) He is calling us to – in actuality – be crucified with Christ, giving up the ghost of our own will and way.

In a posture of utter flatness before the LORD, Paul prayed – **"For this cause I bow my knees unto the Father of our Lord Jesus Christ."** (Eph. 3:14) This is the only posture of the true disciple. His life must be offered daily as a living sacrifice, holy and acceptable unto God (Rom. 12:1). The sinful nature has not been removed from the believer, and will not be until he is with Jesus. It must be kept under subjection to the Spirit (1 Cor. 9:27). We still choose to yield to one or the other – flesh or the Spirit (Rom. 6:16).

There is a war raging in our members, and only one of these two opposing forces will win.

> **"This I say then, Walk in the Spirit, and ye shall not fulfil the lust of the flesh. For the flesh lusteth against the Spirit, and the Spirit against the flesh: and these are contrary the one to the other: so that ye cannot do the things that ye would." Galatians 5:17-18**

PRAYER: *Father, I acknowledge from Your Word that being born in sin after Adam, I am sold under sin and unable to please You, outside of being rescued by You through the redemption that is in Christ alone. At this moment, I cast my wretched and sinful self down upon Your mercy, begging You to change, rescue, deliver,* *and fill me. Grant Your blessing to my life. Take over, Jesus! Into Thine hands I this moment submit my spirit. I love You, LORD Jesus. Amen.*

Capture Points

1. Read and discuss Romans 7:5-25 (KJV recommended).

2. Write out John 3:30 on an index card: **"He must increase, but I must decrease."** (KJV)

3. Spend a moment in specific prayer for each individual in the group to be blessed with the deep conviction to daily cry out to the LORD for Him to increase and for themselves to decrease.

Chapter Eight

The Cross & the Identity of all Saints

"Who hath delivered us from the power of darkness, and hath translated us into the kingdom of his dear Son." Colossians 1:13

We all descend from Adam; therefore we are born in sin, and are in need of God's redemption. Out of the loins of the sons of Noah were overspread the peoples of the whole earth, and in Christ are brought together the eternal people of God – for His good pleasure, redeemed through Christ alone.

There are different colored and shaped stones in the wall that makes up the temple of the LORD, and yet there is one purpose ordained for that body of people He has redeemed (Rom. 8:29).

"Ye also, as lively stones, are built up a spiritual house, an holy priesthood, to offer up spiritual sacrifices, acceptable to God by Jesus Christ ... But ye are a chosen generation, a royal priesthood, an holy nation, a peculiar people; that ye should shew forth the praises of him who hath called you out of darkness into his marvellous light." 1 Peter 2:5, 9

It is the cross that separates us unto God – in His eternal family. When He saves me through **"the blood of his cross,"** He simultaneously then separates me along with every other true believer – whom He has redeemed out of **"every kindred, and tongue, and people, and nation. "** (Rev. 5:9)

The Bible tells us that **"God was in Christ, reconciling the world unto himself,"** and in doing such, He has **"translated us into the kingdom of his dear Son,"** forming one new body in the earth and in Heaven (2 Cor. 5:19; Eph. 2:12-22; Col. 1:13). This Jesus and His body are to be the identity of all of His saints.

> **"But God forbid that I should glory, save (except) in the cross of our Lord Jesus Christ, by whom the world is crucified unto me, and I unto the world." Galatians 6:14**

Paul said he gloried only in Jesus. Who or what do *you* glory in? If you glory in Jesus, then you will of a surety love His people – regardless of their natural heritage.

All the saints of Christ are to **"rejoice in Christ Jesus, and have NO confidence in the flesh."**

> **"For we are the circumcision, which worship God in the spirit, and rejoice in Christ Jesus, and have NO confidence in the flesh." Philippians 3:3**

Christ's true people are to **"have NO confidence"** in their fleshly people group, and to **"know NO man after the flesh."** (2 Cor. 5:16; Phil. 3:3) If I am to **"know no man after the flesh,"** and to **"have no confidence in the flesh,"** then I am to be no respecter of persons as concerning the language they speak, the color of their skin, their body type, the way they dress, their financial status, or any other superficial element (read James 2:1-10).

> "Who shall lay any thing to the charge of God's elect? It is God that justifieth. Who is he that condemneth? It is Christ that died, yea rather, that is risen again, who is even at the right hand of God, who also maketh intercession for us." Romans 8:33-34

The LORD God sees the very attitudes of our hearts, and God forbid that we **"lay anything to the charge of God's elect"** in our attitudes! If God chose them and Christ came and died for them, who in the world do I think I am to discount them! What arrogance! What sinful disposition! What respecter of persons!

The saints of Christ are not to have confidence in or put stock in their earthly nationalities. Each nationality or people group, from which each of us has come, is of Adam and is therefore utterly sinful in nature. There is no salvageable glory to be had in any natural race of men.

In order to give honor to the LORD, would you mind if this writer shared a tad concerning the sanctifying process that has transpired in him by the Holy Spirit? Part of my lineage is from Italy. Have you beheld how proud Italians can be? God is good, and as we submit to His process of the cross, He separates us from all that does not glorify Him – He moves our heart affections from all earthly affinities onto His beloved Son and our eternity with Him.

> "If ye then be risen with Christ, seek those things which are above, where Christ sitteth on the right hand of God. Set your affection on things above, not on things on the earth. For ye are dead, and your life is hid with Christ in God. When Christ, who is our life, shall appear, then shall ye also appear with him in glory." Colossians 3:1-3

As the affections of our hearts are set upon Christ and His eternal things, and **"not on things on the earth,"** including pride in our natural heritage, we are promised that when He appears, we shall **"appear with him in glory."**

God showed His love for all peoples on the day He birthed His Church. He promised to build His Church, and told us that the gates of hell would not prevail against it (Matt. 16:18-19). Gathered together on the Day of Pentecost, the day the New Testament Church was born, were men from all nations.

> **"And there were dwelling at Jerusalem Jews, devout men, out of every nation under heaven." Acts 2:5**

These men, who were saved and filled with the Holy Ghost, brought the Gospel of Christ back to their nations.

The messengers of Christ demonstrated this blind, divine love as they took the Gospel of Jesus to the ends of the known world. They **"turned the world upside down"** by thoroughly preaching to every people group (Acts 17:6). **"They that were scattered abroad went <u>everywhere</u> preaching the word."** (Acts 8:4) Notice that the early believers, when **"scattered abroad,"** went **"everywhere"** – among all peoples, spreading the Gospel of Jesus.

There is only one way into God, Heaven, and His body of believers – Jesus Christ (Jn. 14:6). In Heaven's eyes, we are a new race, made one in and by Christ's cross. Jesus died and brought all non-Jews and Jews into **"one body."** He has made all of us who are His, **"one new man."**

> **"Having abolished in his flesh the enmity, even the law of commandments contained in ordinances; for to make in himself of twain one new man, so making peace." Ephesians 2:15**

The LORD has prepared a new dwelling place for His people (Jn. 14:1-6). We are going to live in a new place all together – the New Jerusalem (Rev. 21).

"For here have we no continuing city (here), but we seek one to come." Hebrews 13:14

There is the clear biblical revelation of the uniqueness of races, and such should never be denied. It is clear that God made each individual person, and each people group, unique. This is according to His perfect wisdom and His handiwork, and the blessedness of it can be seen in each people group or nationality. Listen to Paul's discourse to the peoples as he stood on Mars Hill:

"God that made the world and all things therein, seeing that he is Lord of heaven and earth, dwelleth not in temples made with hands; Neither is worshipped with men's hands, as though he needed any thing, seeing he giveth to all life, and breath, and all things; <u>And hath made of one blood all nations of men for to dwell on all the face of the earth, and hath determined the times before appointed, and the bounds of their habitation;</u> That they should seek the Lord, if haply they might feel after him, and find him, though he be not far from every one of us: For in him we live, and move, and have our being; as certain also of your own poets have said, For we are also his offspring. Forasmuch then as we are the offspring of God ... Because he hath appointed a day, in the which he will judge the world in righteousness by that man whom he hath ordained; whereof he hath given assurance unto all men, in that he hath raised him from the dead." Acts 17:24-31

So denying the uniqueness of each special people group would be to deny reality and cease to be honest in our approach. Yet the body of our LORD, which is **"one body in Christ,"** is made up of peoples from all people groups (1 Cor. 12:5).

By reason of our identity in Jesus Christ, we are brought together by Him into one body. He is our identity, and we are therefore His precious body. It is the cross – the daily dying to the self-life – that will make way for the Holy Spirit to bring forth this revelation in our hearts.

I must die daily to the temptation and to the voices of those who would draw me away from my identity with Christ and His body. I must separate myself from those whose theology doesn't foster a deeper love for Christ and His beloved people – no matter what their rationale.

There is no glory to be had in being proud of our earthly heritage, for we seek a city and country to come, as heavenly citizens, where the LORD Himself is actually and literally going to dwell with us (Rev. 21-22).

> **"For here have we no continuing city, but we seek one to come." Hebrews 13:14**

All else in this brief life should pale in comparison to this glorious truth. Have you read the last 2 chapters of the Bible lately?

Who are we?

> **"For we are the circumcision, which worship God in the spirit, and rejoice in Christ Jesus, and have no confidence in the flesh." Philippians 3:3**

Beloved, it is **"the cross of our LORD Jesus Christ"** that we should glory in (Gal. 6:14).

"But God forbid that I should glory, save in the cross of our Lord Jesus Christ, by whom the world is crucified unto me, and I unto the world." Galatians 6:14

While many in leadership today write and stand up in earthly pride for their race or heritage, to declare their convoluted and erroneous theology, the apostle Paul **"determined not to know any thing among you, save Jesus Christ, and him crucified."** (1 Cor. 2:2)

When Paul spoke to the believers at the town of Corinth, he declared:

"For I determined not to know any thing among you, save Jesus Christ, and him crucified." 1 Corinthians 2:2

The preacher of the Word of God must denounce all that does not glorify Jesus Christ.

"Therefore seeing we have this ministry, as we have received mercy, we faint not; <u>But have renounced the hidden things of dishonesty, not walking in craftiness, nor handling the word of God deceitfully; but by manifestation of the truth</u> commending ourselves to every man's conscience in the sight of God." 2 Corinthians 4:1-2

The eternal souls of men are at stake, and Satan diverts those teachers whose hearts are not truly seeking Him who is the truth, inspiring them to preach **"another gospel"** and lead many astray (2 Cor. 11:2-5; Gal. 1:6-9). These false prophets are totally un-Christlike; they are hate-mongers and **"accursed,"** and should be openly rejected and exposed (Rom. 16:17-18; Eph. 5:11; Gal. 1:8-9; 1 Jn. 4:1; 2 Jn. 7-11).

There are but 2 clearly divided kingdoms: God's and Satan's. Christ's cross rescues men from Satan's kingdom, and brings them into God's kingdom. Satan seeks to further divide the peoples of the earth into other groups and factions, doing what he does – stealing, killing, and destroying (Jn. 10:10). In fact, Jesus foretold us that in the final days of this age, just before His return, **"nation shall rise against nation, and kingdom against kingdom."** (Matt. 24:7)

The Greek word for **"nation"** here is *ethnos* and refers to a people group. Not only is Satan's plan to pit geographic nation against nation, but also people group against people group that dwell in the same geographic area. This should be easily observed.

In this following passage, remember that the **"Gentiles"** represent EVERY non-Jew. In your personal study, you will do well to pore over Ephesians 2. Here's a portion:

> **"And you hath he quickened, who were dead in trespasses and sins ... Wherefore remember, that ye being in time past Gentiles in the flesh, who are called Uncircumcision by that which is called the Circumcision in the flesh made by hands; That at that time ye were without Christ, being aliens from the commonwealth of Israel, and strangers from the covenants of promise, having no hope, and without God in the world: But now in Christ Jesus ye who sometimes were far off are made nigh by the blood of Christ. For he is our peace, who hath made both one, and hath broken down the middle wall of partition between us; Having abolished in his flesh the enmity, even the law of commandments contained in ordinances; for to make in himself of twain one new man, so making peace; And that he might reconcile both unto God in one body by the cross, having slain the enmity thereby: And came and preached peace to you**

> which were afar off, and to them that were nigh. <u>For
> through him we both have access by one Spirit unto
> the Father.</u> Now therefore ye are no more strangers
> and foreigners, but fellowcitizens with the saints,
> and of the household of God; And are built upon
> the foundation of the apostles and prophets, Jesus
> Christ himself being the chief corner stone; In
> whom ye also are builded together for an habitation
> of God through the Spirit." Ephesians 2:1, 11-22

There are only 2 kingdoms in the earth – Christ's and
Satan's. Jesus said **"He that is not with me, IS against me."**
(Matt. 12:30) Read that one again. Memorize it. Do Jesus'
words need a man to decipher? I think not. They are self-
interpretive, and as our LORD promised, the Holy Spirit
will teach them to all who are His (Jn. 14:26; 16:13).

Those who are **"with"** Christ, having been born again into
Him, His salvation, and family, are **"one body in Christ"**;
and are living to worship Him alone, and to bring other
men into His kingdom (Rom. 12:5). All men are eternal
souls that Jesus died for, and He told us He desires that
they **"all"** come to repentance and be saved (1 Tim. 2:4; 2
Pet. 3:9; 1 Jn. 2:2). God bless each of us to love ALL His
precious saints, showing no partiality. *Father, please rid us
of ungodly discriminations and make us pure in heart, Jesus! We
beg You now, LORD, to grant our hearts the purity that comes
with Your wisdom. Amen.*

> "But the wisdom that is from above is first pure,
> then peaceable, gentle, and easy to be intreated,
> full of mercy and good fruits, without partiality,
> and without hypocrisy." James 3:17

"ONE Body in Christ"

> "So we, being many, are one body in Christ, and
> every one members one of another." Romans 12:5

For Jews and ALL others, there is only one way to enter God's kingdom and we are thereby **"one body in Christ."**

"Seeing it is one God, which shall justify the circumcision (Jews) by faith, and uncircumcision (non-Jews) through faith." Romans 3:30

Satan would use clever speaking men to draw us away from what God told us in His Word. These men with feigned words deceive the hearts of the simple (unlearned), drawing them away from pure devotion to Christ and loving His body, to earthly affinities.

As His **"one body in Christ,"** we are to **"stand fast in one spirit, with one mind striving together for the faith of the gospel."** (Rom. 12:5; Phil. 1:27)

Today, the promised multiplicity and onslaught of deceivers takes many shapes, sizes, and colors (2 Tim. 3:13). There are many who fill pulpits and minds with a message of hate, feigning to represent the LORD and yet, preaching an insidious hatred in their messages. Take for example the white supremacists groups who use the Bible, and the black pastors who preach a black liberation theology. Both are of Satan and not Christ. They are scattering abroad people – directing them onto earthly affinities and not fostering in them a love for Christ and His **"one body."** (Matt. 12:30; Rom. 12:5)

This sinful and diabolical hate exists not only between different people groups, but also among peoples. There are different tribes of the brown, yellow, black, red, and white races that possess and perpetrate enmity against one another. But the Bible says that **"God is love"** and **"He that loveth not knoweth not God."** (1 Jn. 4:8)

The true servant of Jesus loves all men **"without partiality"** and fosters in others a rich and divine love for all men, especially those who are **"of the household of faith."** (Gal. 6:10; James 3:17)

> **"As we have therefore opportunity, let us do good unto all men, especially unto them who are of the household of faith." Galatians 6:10**

Why did God send us His only begotten Son?

> **"For God so loved the world, that he gave his only begotten Son, that whosoever believeth in him should not perish, but have everlasting life." John 3:16**

The Father sent the Son because He loves all men, right? Do we love all men?

Did Jesus come to save brown sinners or just yellow sinners, white or black sinners?

> **"Christ Jesus came into the world to save sinners; of whom I am chief." 1 Timothy 1:15**

> **"And he is the propitiation (atoning sacrifice) for our sins: and not for ours only, but also for the sins of <u>the whole world</u>." 1 John 2:2**

At the announcement of the birth of Jesus, God made His intentions known:

> **"Glory to God in the highest, and on earth peace, <u>good will toward men</u>." Luke 2:14**

The LORD has **"good will toward men,"** and so should and will all of His true children. Love is the earmark fruit of all who truly know the LORD. Hatred and those who possess it – whether hidden or not – will not enter His holy Heaven.

> "We know that we have passed from death unto life, because we love the brethren. He that loveth not his brother abideth in death. Whosoever hateth his brother is a murderer: and ye know that no murderer hath eternal life abiding in him." 1 John 3:14-15

Deceivers today foster in their audiences a pride in their natural heritage instead of preaching the pure Word of God, which teaches us that Christ died for all men, and when He saves them, He brings them all together into **"one body."** The true disciple of the Son of God identifies with Jesus Christ, is dead to self and his own agenda, and walks in His love. He loves and honors every member of the body that Jesus, with His own sinless blood, **"hast redeemed us to God by thy blood out of every kindred, and tongue, and people, and nation."**

Revelation 5:9-10 says:

> "And they sung a new song, saying, Thou art worthy to take the book, and to open the seals thereof: for thou wast slain, and hast redeemed us to God by thy blood out of every kindred, and tongue, and people, and nation. And hast made us unto our God kings and priests: and we shall reign on the earth."

Being dead with Christ, buried to the old man and all of its earthly identifications, Paul had to denounce any loyalty or affinity of his Jewish heritage – **"But what things were gain to me, those I counted loss for Christ. Yea doubtless, and I count all things but loss for the excellency of the knowledge of Christ Jesus my Lord: for whom I have suffered the loss of all things, and do count them but dung, that I may win Christ ... That I may know him, and the power of his resurrection, and the fellowship of**

his sufferings, being made conformable unto his death."
(Phil. 3:7-10)

Like the apostle Paul, all who are in Christ are severed from
all other affinities and identified with Him in His sufferings,
death, burial, and resurrection. Their whole life pursuit and
goal is to **"know Him."** In knowing Him who **"is love,"**
His genuine disciples love all men.

"The blood of his cross" redeems us from sin, self, Satan,
and hatred or partiality (Col. 1:20). The mind or thinking of
all true disciples of Jesus must be transformed to conform to
His revealed heart of love toward all men (Rom. 12:2). This
will certainly occur as we **"present (y)our bodies a living
sacrifice, holy and acceptable unto God."** (Rom. 12:1)

In light of these prevalent biblical truths, we must see all
men as eternal souls for whom Jesus came and bled, and
love them with His love. When we are, by His Holy Spirit,
granted this understanding, His love will fill our hearts,
breaking down the walls of hatred built by Satan and the
lies of sinful men. The love of Christ demonstrates itself as
His people fellowship, and with His love in them, dwell
with and **"love one another."** The love of Christ that fills
the hearts of His people, is a sign and wonder to the world
– **"A new commandment I give unto you, That ye love one
another; as I have loved you, that ye also love one another.
By this shall all men know that ye are my disciples, if ye
have love one to another."** (Jn. 13:34-35)

> **"For there is no respect of persons with God."
> Romans 2:11**
>
> **"God accepteth no man's person." Galatians 2:6**

In God's holy eyes, those who hate (for any reason) are
murderers and do not possess eternal life (1 Jn. 3:14-15).

Having respect of persons is sin and will exclude one from God's eternal kingdom.

> **"But if ye have respect to persons, ye commit sin, and are convinced of the law as transgressors." James 2:9**

According to Proverbs 6:16-17, **"a proud look"** or looking down on someone else, is **"an abomination"** to the LORD.

If you somehow believe you are better than another of less fortunate circumstances or another race, you are utterly deceived and should seek the LORD for His gift of repentance.

> **"Be of the same mind one toward another. Mind not high things, but condescend to men of low estate. Be not wise in your own conceits." Romans 12:16**

Individuals of people groups are not to vaunt themselves in thought, word, attitude, or deed. This is sin in the eyes of a holy God and Judge, and will be punished. Natural Gentiles (all races other than Jews) are not to be **"highminded"** towards other people groups – **"thou standest by faith. Be not highminded, but fear."** (Rom. 11:20) Each individual saint is called to fear before the LORD and be ever thankful for His **"unspeakable gift"** of eternal life, whereby we look for the soon return of Jesus and the **"new Jerusalem"** as we **"rejoice with joy unspeakable and full of glory."** (2 Cor. 9:15; 1 Pet. 1:8; Rev. 3:12; 21:2)

Melissa Robinson writes:

> "Love for one's heritage is just another idol - to be counted as dung - for the sake of knowing Christ. And that includes the idol of American patriotism, especially now that her evil fruits have filled the whole world with their stench. I love these verses from Heb. 11:

9 By faith <u>he sojourned in the land of promise,</u> <u>as in a strange country,</u> dwelling in tabernacles with Isaac and Jacob, the heirs with him of the same promise ...

10 <u>For he looked for a city which hath</u> <u>foundations, whose builder and maker is</u> <u>God</u> ... 13 These all died in faith, not having received the promises, but having seen them afar off, and were persuaded of them, and embraced them, and <u>confessed that they were</u> <u>strangers and pilgrims on the earth.</u>

14 For they that say such things declare plainly that they seek a country.

15 And truly, if they had been mindful of that country from whence they came out, they might have had opportunity to have returned.

16 <u>But now they desire a better country, that is,</u> <u>an heavenly: wherefore God is not ashamed</u> <u>to be called their God: for he hath prepared</u> <u>for them a city.</u>

Wow. Abraham counted even his 'land of promise' as a 'strange country'! He knew that was not the final goal. Those who desire 'a better country' have a city prepared for them, and God is not ASHAMED to be called their God!

Is God ashamed to be called the God of those who cling to and blindly defend their earthly nations?

I can tell you what I am looking for: the Jerusalem above."

As with Paul, God will have to knock some off their high horse of pride, humbling them under His mighty hand, ridding their hearts of every vestige of respecting persons and pride in temporal affinities (Acts 9).

The cross of Christ purchased our salvation and separates us to Christ and away from the pride of men in their own natural people group. We are one eternal body in Jesus and will spend eternity with Him in the New Jerusalem, but only as we persevere in His grace and love to the end (Matt. 10:22; 1 Pet. 2:5, 9; Rev. 21).

> **"This people have I formed for myself; they shall shew forth my praise." Isaiah 43:21**

"God is love" and He requires that we know Him deeply enough to **"walk in love,"** otherwise we shall be cut off from His eternal kingdom (Eph. 5:1-2).

Memory Verse: **"So we, being many, are one body in Christ, and every one members one of another." Romans 12:5**

PRAYER: *Precious LORD Jesus, thank You for making peace between God and men by the blood of Your cross, and for redeeming people from all nations and kingdoms and heritages. Thank You for coming to die for the sins of all men—including me, the very worst of vile sinners! I repent of any partiality in my heart toward any people group that You have created, and for disparaging Your beloved creation. Thank You, LORD, for forgiving my innumerable sins against Thee. Here and now I forgive all who have sinned against me and my people in the past. I love You, Jesus. Set me apart and fill me with Thy holy love. I here and now denounce any prejudice or partiality towards any people group and beg You to fill my heart with Your impartial love—towards all men. Amen.*

Capture Points

1. Write out on an index card and discuss Galatians 6:14 (KJV recommended).

2. Write out Hebrews 13:14 on an index card for personal absorption (KJV recommended).

3. Discuss Philippians 1:27-29. Make sure to read this passage carefully and prayerfully. There will be several truth points of interest (KJV recommended).

4. Discuss Romans 12:16 (KJV recommended).

Chapter Nine

The Cross & the Wolf

"There is a conspiracy of her prophets in the midst thereof, like a roaring lion ravening the prey; they have devoured souls; they have taken the treasure and precious things; they have made her many widows in the midst thereof. Her priests have violated my law, and have profaned mine holy things: they have put no difference between the holy and profane, neither have they shown *difference* between the unclean and the clean, and have hid their eyes from my sabbaths, and I am profaned among them. Her princes in the midst thereof *are* like wolves ravening the prey, to shed blood, *and* to destroy souls, to get dishonest gain." Ezekiel 22:25-27

Make no mistake: there is a literal **"conspiracy"** of the false prophets against the God they claim to be serving. In their rebellion **"they have devoured souls."** They have removed the **"treasure and precious things"** of God's Word by replacing His precious precepts with the use of fad books, human philosophy, psychologies, and traditions. In doing so they have spoiled many souls, a fate of which Paul warned us to **"Beware."** (Col. 2:8). This they do to **"get dishonest gain"** – to gain their own fame, man's approval, and earthly riches.

At the center of the **"precious things"** stolen by today's wolves is the biblical message of the cross of Christ – how that Christ laid down His life on the altar of the cross for our redemption, and then commands those who will be His to lay down their own lives to follow Him (Matt. 16:24-25; Lk. 9:23-24).

The false teacher conveys to people what they want to hear in order to become popular. He meticulously picks and chooses the Scriptures he uses in order to entice and allure his audience to be endeared to him – in order **"to get dishonest gain."** (Ezek. 22:27) He refuses to teach the things that would jeopardize his standing with people. He fears men and not God (Gal. 1:10). This method of only teaching soft and dainty things works due to the obvious fact that there are so many who want to be told that going to Heaven and Christianity are easy. But that is simply a misrepresentation. That's not what Jesus and His apostles taught.

> **"Strive (agonize) to enter in at the strait gate: for many, I say unto you, will seek to enter in, and shall not be able." Luke 13:24**

Does that sound easy?

> **"Confirming the souls of the disciples, *and* exhorting them to continue in the faith, and that <u>we must through much tribulation enter into the kingdom of God.</u>" Acts 14:22**

> **"Yea, and all that will live godly in Christ Jesus shall suffer persecution." 2 Timothy 3:12**

How many times are you hearing these divinely inspired words communicated by your leader(s)? These are the divinely-inspired words spoken by Jesus Christ and the apostle Paul.

What about the following words of Christ? Have you heard this preached lately?

> **"Enter ye in at the strait gate: for wide *is* the gate, and broad *is* the way, that leadeth to destruction, and many there be which go in thereat: Because strait *is* the gate, and narrow *is* the way, which leadeth unto life, and few there be that find it. Beware of false prophets, which come to you in sheep's clothing, but inwardly they are ravening wolves." Matthew 7:13-15**

Notice in the above passage what Jesus is telling us. There is a narrow way that leads to Heaven and a wide road that leads to hell. Many are going down that wide road that leads to damnation and only a few are going down the narrow road that leads to eternal life. **"False prophets"** who are disguised in **"sheep's clothing"** are, by their refusal to teach what Jesus taught, making the road to Heaven appear wider than He said it is.

The wolf leader is a hireling who is using his position in the ministry as a business to promote himself, so he does not want God's Word getting in the way of such "success." He certainly does not want God's pure and circumcising Word of the cross doing its convicting work, because that won't garner to him masses of people to fulfill his personal, self-serving dream. The counterfeit leader would rather be relevant, relative, and seeker-sensitive in order to reach a much larger segment of society. He markets his cross-less wares to the vast majority of people who are self-seeking instead of Savior-seeking (Matt. 7:13-14; 2 Tim. 3:1-7). The beguiling author or leader targets this rebellious audience because they are much more plentiful and don't read and heed the Bible, and therefore are easy to deceive and employ for the accomplishment of his goal.

Those who serve the lusts of the flesh instead of Christ desire to be told that they are doing good in their current spiritual state, as they indulge in the lusts of the sinful nature, all the while believing they are saved and going to Heaven. But the Bible tells us that all those who love this world and the things in it are not of the Father (1 Jn. 2:15-17). They shun the light of truth coming from the true God-fearing remnant of God's people. They come to the defense of their false leaders when watchmen seek to uncover their evil teachings that are contrary to the clear message of God's Word.

> **"And this is the condemnation, that light is come into the world, and men loved darkness rather than light, because their deeds were evil. For every one that doeth evil hateth the light, neither cometh to the light, lest his deeds should be reproved. But he that doeth truth cometh to the light, that his deeds may be made manifest, that they are wrought in God." John 3:19-21**

Of the **"evil workers"** who **"mind earthly things,"** the Holy Spirit warns:

> **"(For many walk, of whom I have told you often, and now tell you even weeping, that they are the enemies of the cross of Christ: Whose end is destruction, whose God is their belly, and whose glory is in their shame, <u>who mind earthly things</u>.)" Philippians 3:18-19**

The wolf entices people to act on their sinful lusts – covetousness, greed, spiritual adultery, and idolatry. Instead of preaching the cross – that we *must* die that He might live, they **"mind earthly things."** They tend to teach and talk about the things of this world. The false prophet completely ignores such an essential truth – he is an enemy **"of the cross of Christ."** (Phil. 3:18) He himself does not bear the cross so he naturally doesn't teach others to deny the self-life, take up the cross, and follow Jesus. In neglecting to teach the cross, he teaches **"another gospel"** which is **"any other gospel"** that is not the original Gospel given to us by Christ and His holy apostles (2 Cor. 11:2-4; Gal. 1:6-9; Jude 3-4). The false gospel message of the wolf leader is void of the cross, and any cross-less gospel is a counterfeit gospel.

The cross-less leader actually cheats his audience out of hearing the vital message of the death-to-self; if they could but learn to die to self for the Savior, it would facilitate for them rich spiritual fellowship with Him (Phil. 3:10).

Getting saved is the entrance point into God's kingdom and not the ending point. That one which will be an overcomer and **"endure to the end,"** must obey Jesus in abstaining from serving himself so that he can please the LORD (Matt. 10:22; Lk. 9:23-24; Rev. 2-3). This is what it means to deny ourselves and take up our crosses to follow Him. Jesus said, **"If any man will come after me, let him deny himself, and take up his cross, and follow me."** (Matt. 16:24)

The wolf leader is identified by the personal carnality he walks in (Jude 3-19). He is self-indulgent (Isa. 56:10-12; Phil. 3:18-19; 2 Pet. 2:19). He spends more time on self-interests and minding earthly things than he does giving himself **"continually to prayer, and to the ministry of the word."** (Acts 6:4) He is not prepared to be empowered and led by the Holy Spirit in order to preach God's Word to feed His sheep. Being entangled in the things of this world has precluded him from having time to watch over the souls of the sheep of Christ's pasture (Prov. 27:23; Jer. 23:1-2; 1 Pet.

5:1-6). By definition, this kind of leader is a hireling, and not a true shepherd. Therefore, Jesus' followers today should not submit to him according to Hebrews 13:7 & 17.

Paul, a known true servant and apostle of Christ, said:

> **"For our conversation is in heaven; from whence also we look for the Saviour, the Lord Jesus Christ: Who shall change our vile body, that it may be fashioned like unto his glorious body, according to the working whereby he is able even to subdue all things unto himself." Philippians 3:20-21**

God is going to do His will in the life of the one who seeks Him with a whole heart daily (Jer. 29:13). The true disciple cleanses his heart daily, putting aside his own will so that the LORD's perfect will can prevail (Jer. 4:14; Matt. 5:8; 2 Cor. 7:1; 2 Tim. 2:21). Cry out to Him now in utter desperation, announcing to Him what He has told us – that you have no hope without Him and can do nothing of eternal value without Him (Jn. 15:5). We have nothing, can do nothing, and are nothing without Jesus Christ – **"For of him (Christ), and through him, and to him, are all things: to whom be glory for ever. Amen."** (Rom. 11:36)

The beloved and late A. W. Tozer stated:

> "There must be a work of God in destruction before we are free. We must invite the cross to do its deadly work within us. We must bring our self-sins to the cross of judgment."

The Word of God instructs us to **"examine"** and **"judge"** ourselves so that we will be in check with God, and not ultimately found guilty of serving self and not the Savior (1 Cor. 11:31-32; 2 Cor. 13:5).

> **"For if we would judge ourselves, we should not be judged. But when we are judged, we are chastened**

of the Lord, that we should not be condemned with the world." 1 Corinthians 11:31-32

There will be many surprised on Judgment Day (Matt. 7:22-23). They will be those who refused to build their lives on the Word – hearing and obeying it (Matt. 7:21-29; James 1:22).

Those who don't want to die to the self-life have made many wolves very popular. This demonstrates several things, including the sad truth that most people aren't willing to put themselves aside that Jesus might reign (2 Cor. 4:10-12). These are those whom He told us have a mere **"form of godliness, but denying the power thereof."** To the remnant He says, **"from such turn away."** (2 Tim. 3:5)

Paul instructed his understudy, Timothy, to **"Preach the word."** He then said that **"the time will come when they will not endure sound doctrine; but after their own lusts shall they heap to themselves teachers, having itching ears. And they shall turn away *their* ears from the truth, and shall be turned unto fables."** (2 Tim. 4:2-4)

To **"endure sound doctrine"** is to take God at His Word and never dodge biblical truth that is not flattering to the flesh and requires death to self. Those who **"will not endure sound doctrine"** in this fleeting life will forever regret their short lived self-indulgence. Remember Esau, who traded his eternal birthright for a quick fix bowl of soup?

> **"And make straight paths for your feet, lest that which is lame be turned out of the way; but let it rather be healed. Follow peace with all *men*, and holiness, without which no man shall see the Lord: Looking diligently lest any man fail of the grace of God; lest any root of bitterness springing up trouble *you*, and thereby many be defiled; Lest there *be* any fornicator, or profane person, as Esau, who for one**

morsel of meat sold his birthright. For ye know how that afterward, when he would have inherited the blessing, he was rejected: for he found no place of repentance, though he sought it carefully with tears." Hebrews 12:13-17

The cross and the wolf are mutually exclusive. Though good at feigning adherence to the gospel, the wolf does not honor Christ's death and the **"blood of his cross,"** nor does he take up the cross daily, denying his own self-serving and sinful nature (Col. 1:20). Due to his own personal disobedience, he naturally can't lead others down the narrow road that leads to life.

The wicked one and his accomplices have targeted the very people of God. They have stricken at the heart of the Gospel – the cross.

"... the enemy hath done wickedly in the sanctuary. Thine enemies roar in the midst of thy congregations; they set up their ensigns *for* signs... They have cast fire into thy sanctuary, they have defiled *by casting down* the dwellingplace of thy name to the ground." Psalms 74:3-4, 7

The enemy has attacked the very **"sanctuary"** of the LORD by setting up his own ensigns or name in place of Christ, and has cast into our midst the strange fire doctrines of a cross-less gospel which is no gospel at all.

On the merit of **"the blood of his cross,"** the believer is **"complete in him."** (Col. 1:20; 2:9) The wolf is the child of the enemy, who has come to steal, kill, and destroy (Jn. 10:10). In the midst of the sanctuary, the wolf has stolen the place and position due only to Christ, who alone is worthy to reign as LORD over His people, which He purchased **"by himself"** with His very own blood (Heb. 1:3). In doing so, he has cut off the flow of nourishment from Christ – the

"Head" of the Church – to His body (Col. 2:18-19). This is what being spoiled is – when the very **"reward"** Christ died to purchase for us is stolen by those who would **"beguile you with enticing words."** (Col. 2:3, 18). We are only complete in Christ and partake of the treasures of His wisdom as we worship Him in Spirit and in truth, upholding Him alone as our object of worship (Jn. 4:23-24; Col. 2:3-19).

Wolf leaders do not like the cross, which dictates that they must truly repent and die to all self-ambition, and allow Christ alone to be glorified in their own lives and in the midst of His people. They desire to use people to make themselves look good to others, so they compel their prey to do things outwardly to accomplish this. They do this to escape **"persecution for the cross of Christ."**

> **"As many as desire to make a fair shew in the flesh, they constrain (compel) you to be circumcised; only lest they should suffer persecution for the cross of Christ." Galatians 6:12**

At all cost, the counterfeit will seek to evade and avoid the suffering associated with **"persecution for the cross of Christ."** He therefore creates a church environment where he makes people feel good about themselves, but he refuses to live and preach the cross to prepare them to meet Christ as His bride (Matt. 25:1-13; Eph. 5:25-27; Rev. 19:7).

Of these leaders, Paul writes in the very next verse:

> **"For neither they themselves who are circumcised keep the law; but desire to have you circumcised, that they may glory in your flesh. But God forbid that I should glory, save in the cross of our Lord Jesus Christ, by whom the world is crucified unto me, and I unto the world." Galatians 6:13-14**

There are many modern day forms of circumcision (outward religion that is void of repentance, regeneration, vital relationship, and a life that glorifies God in the spirit first). The wolf leaders, who glory in self and in religion, are glad to have people patronizing their church businesses and making them feel good about themselves as they look out from their ivory pulpits and see people approving them by their presence and/or participation. But they don't care for your soul – **"What shall a man give in exchange for his soul?"** (Mk. 8:37) What will the devoured souls say in eternity? What will be the cry of those who were destroyed by the wolves? Will they say like Psalms 142:4, **"No man cared for my soul?"** It will be too late then.

That's what a wolf is – someone who is in the ministry in order to get personal gain and not to love Christ and diligently watch for the souls of His precious flock. Therefore he builds his own ministry instead of being used by the LORD to build His Church (Matt. 16:18; 2 Cor. 4:10-12).

Of many who hold positions of spiritual leadership, Jesus says:

> **"For they loved the praise of men more than the praise of God." John 12:43**

The religion taught by these beguilers is not genuine Christianity. Jesus promised persecution to those who would follow Him (Matt. 5:10-12). Exchanging identity with Christ Himself and alone for some other religious affinity insulates people from persecution. In turn, being kept from persecution insulates people from crucially identifying with the Person, Jesus Christ. People are taught to glory in the fleshly things like "I'm Baptist," "I'm Charismatic," or "I'm Methodist." This idolatrous identification intercepts the affections of their hearts from Christ, the One they should be looking to and upon whom they should be setting their heart affections (Col. 3:1-4).

> **"Now this I say, that every one of you saith, I am of Paul; and I of Apollos; and I of Cephas; and I of Christ. Is Christ divided? was Paul crucified for you? or were ye baptized in the name of Paul? ... For the preaching of the cross is to them that perish foolishness; but unto us which are saved it is the power of God." 1 Corinthians 1:12-13, 18**

Even those in the church world who have leadership positions are seen here to be perishing. They count **"the preaching of the cross"** as **"foolishness."** If they didn't, they would preach the cross of which Paul said, **"But God forbid that I should glory, save in the cross of our Lord Jesus Christ, by whom the world is crucified unto me, and I unto the world."** (Gal. 6:14)

Paul understood that there could be no raising up until there was first a laying down of the life in death and burial (Jn. 12:24; 1 Cor. 15:36).

The Pharisees lived in the flesh. They sought the praises of men and not God (Matt. 23; Jn. 12:43). The fleshly nature loves this type of identification – the praises of mere men – because being a Methodist or Baptist doesn't offend people and keeps life smooth. However, being a follower of Jesus Christ does convict others and brings persecution upon the true disciple (2 Tim. 3:12). The name of Jesus Christ is powerful, and those who love Him confess Him and receive persecution as He promised (Matt. 10:22; Lk. 12:8-9; 2 Tim. 3:12).

The false gospel that is preached by so many today is obviously counterfeit to those who read their Bibles daily. This fairytale gospel of today tells us that God wants us to prosper in all ways while escaping all trials, tribulation, hardships, and suffering of any kind. Instead of God's Word being their theology, they say in their mythology that the LORD is only on His holy throne to help us get a good parking spot, and make us happy so we can have our best life now. The Bible truth is that God is interested in our best life *then* and not *now*, and this comes from laying down our lives – decreasing daily – that Jesus might increase (Jn. 3:30). Eternal blessings are just that – forever, and knowing Christ guarantees them. Not knowing Him guarantees eternally conscious suffering. Those who genuinely know the LORD are busy laying down their lives, learning to love Him more, and being a blessing to others. Along the path in this life we too will be blessed, but not to the fulfillment of our depraved self-serving flesh that is here today and gone tomorrow (James 4:14). The Bible tells us to lay up our treasure in Heaven not on earthly things. We need to get that in our spirits and understand the amazing plan that God has for our eternal future, while not being seduced by leaders to **"mind earthly things."** (Phil. 3:19)

Religion and those wolves who perpetrate it upon people, provides a comfortable place for the deceitful heart, never calling it to repent and bring forth **"fruits meet for (consistent with) repentance."** (Matt. 3:2, 7-8, 10) Doing good works and following an outward form of godliness cloaks the sinful heart, because it does not demand full repentance like the original Gospel does (Mk. 6:12; Lk. 13:3, 5; 24:47; Acts 3:19).

These things are not being pointed out to merely identify the many wolves operating in our midst, but more importantly to warn the individual reader who would desire to follow Christ. Many warnings are found in Scripture concerning being aware of and escaping the lure of the evil one, who uses men to lead astray **"many."**

PRAYER: *Father, please grant me eye salve to see Your holy truth and the many wolves that now are disguised in sheep's clothing and leading many to hell. Help me, Jesus! I this moment turn afresh to You fully, asking You to have mercy on me and wash away all my sins. Grant the eyes of my heart discernment as only You can, as I walk closely with You. I choose this day to deny my own self will and desires and ask You to consume me with Your wisdom, power, and grace. LORD Jesus, please bless me to know You intimately. Amen.*

Capture Points

1. Read and discuss Ezekiel 22:25-27 and talk about the danger of false leaders, and Satan's intention and goal of devouring and destroying souls through them (KJV recommended).

2. Read and discuss Philippians 3:18-19.

3. Read and discuss Psalms 74:3-4, 7. Pay close attention to the targeting of and penetration into the congregation of the LORD by the enemy of souls.

4. Write out on an index card and discuss John 12:43: **"For they loved the praise of men more than the praise of God."** (KJV recommended)

Chapter Ten

"Them that Seduce You"
1 John 2:24

"He saved others; himself he cannot save. If he be the King of Israel, let him now come down from the cross, and we will believe him." Matthew 27:42

"Come down from the cross" is the cry of the enemy of all souls. Here he inspired God-less men to tempt Christ to not complete the work of redemption. In the same way, today, God-less pulpiteers and writers say nothing of the daily cross Christ commanded to be taken up by any person who would follow Him (Lk. 9:23-24).

Peter himself reviled Jesus when Christ told him He would be going to the cross. Jesus attributed that work to **"Satan."** When Peter, being used of Satan spoke, the Son of God **"turned, and said unto Peter, Get thee behind me, Satan: thou art an offence unto me: for thou savourest not the things that be of God, but those that be of men. Then said Jesus unto his disciples, If any *man* will come after me, let him deny himself, and take up his cross, and follow me. For whosoever will save his life shall lose it: and whosoever will lose his life for my sake shall find**

it. For what is a man profited, if he shall gain the whole world, and lose his own soul? or what shall a man give in exchange for his soul?" (Matt. 16:23-26)

Here Jesus spoke not only of the necessity of His own redeeming cross, but also of the daily cross to be taken up by each and every one of those who would follow Him. This should forever underscore and cement in our understanding the necessity of the daily cross.

> "Galatians 2:20 says, 'I am crucified with Christ,' and Rom 6:5 says, 'For if we have been planted (united) together in the likeness of His death.' These are both in the Greek perfect verb tense. This indicates a past event WITH CONTINUING EFFECTS. So, it could literally say 'I have been and continue to be crucified with Christ' and 'For if we have been and continue to be planted ....' Romans 8:36, 2 Corinthians 4:10, and 1 Corinthians 15:31 clearly speak of a daily death with Christ. Ephesians 4:22-24 talks of a continual putting off (death) of the old man, as does 2 Corinthians 4:16. Martin Luther taught of a daily Spirit baptism and called it 'dying upward.' These people who teach otherwise resist the daily cross. This is the error of triumphalism.
>
> As we appropriate the finished work daily, we become more and more what we already are. We possess our possessions. Compare Colossians 3:3 with Colossians 3:5." Travis Bryan III

Let's take brother Bryan's advice and put together verses 3 and 5 of Colossians 3:

> **"For ye are dead, and your life is hid with Christ in God ... Mortify therefore your members which are upon the earth; fornication, uncleanness, inordinate**

affection, evil concupiscence, and covetousness, which is idolatry."

T. Austin-Sparks stated the following:

> "We have not to die; we are dead. What we have to do is to accept our death ... In baptism ... we simply step in there and say, 'That position which God has settled with reference to me is the one which I now accept, and I testify here in this way to the fact that I have accepted God's position for me, namely, that in the Cross I have been brought to an end.'"

The true disciple is always **"delivered unto death for Jesus' sake."** (2 Cor 4:11) He has **"crucified the flesh with the affections and lusts."** (Gal. 5:24) He is daily putting to death **"the deeds of the body"** and being **"raised up"** by the power of the same Holy Spirit **"that raised up Christ from the dead."** (Rom. 8:11, 13) He rejoices in **"Christ Jesus"** and has **"no confidence in the flesh."** (Phil. 3:3)

> **"I die daily"** – **"Always bearing about in the body the dying of the Lord Jesus, that the life also of Jesus might be made manifest in our body. For we which live are always delivered unto death for Jesus' sake** ... **that the life also of Jesus might be made manifest in our mortal flesh. So then death worketh in us, but life in you." 1 Corinthians 15:31; 2 Corinthians 4:10-12**

Concerning the raising up process of the Gospel of God, T. Austin-Sparks wrote:

> "The unalterable basis of an open heaven is a grave, and a crisis at which you come to an end of your own self-life. It is the crisis of real experiential identification with Christ in His death."

Though we entered into His death upon initial salvation, accepting and experiencing that death is still a daily choice, an individual decision to be made on an ongoing basis. One's choice to continue to persevere, following Christ as He clearly prescribed, will determine his eternal destination (Lk. 9:62; 19:13; 21:19; Gal. 6:7-9).

The insidious circumventing of the cross can come in many clandestine ways that are masked with pious outer garb. Today, while refusing to utter the full counsel of the One they claim to be representing, smiling and charismatic men stand in sheep's clothing, promising heavenly life to those who live in sin. They only prosper due to the volitional biblical illiteracy of the masses. Ignorance of the truth is a choice with eternal consequences (Hos. 4:6; Matt. 22:29; 2 Thess. 2:10-12).

Many like to hide behind works they do in and surrounding their local church home. They relish singing in the choir, ushering, doing drama or being a part of the technical team, helping in various ways, or even preaching a message, and yet the life of Christ is not manifesting in their personal lives as they go out into their world daily. His light in them is not bright enough to shine into the darkened hearts of men through personal evangelism. They have been steeped in a mere form or formula of godliness that does not manifest the evidential fruit of one who is truly in Christ, radiant by His glory, and flourishing in His life. A. W. Tozer wrote:

> "Another substitute for discipleship is: *Our Lord referred to this when He reproached the Pharisees for their habit of tithing mint and anise and cumin while at the same time omitting the weightier matters of the Law such as justice, mercy and faith. Literalism manifests itself among us in many ways, but it can always be identified in that it lives by the letter of the Word while ignoring its spirit. It habitually fails to apprehend the inward meaning*

of Christ's words, and contents itself with external compliance with the text. If Christ commands baptism, for instance, it finds fulfillment in the act of water baptism, but the radical meaning of the act as explained in Romans 6 is completely overlooked. It reads the Scriptures regularly, contributes consistently to religious work, attends church every Sunday and otherwise carries on the common duties of a Christian and for this it is to be commended. Its tragic breakdown is its failure to comprehend the Lordship of Christ, the believer's discipleship, separation from the world and the crucifixion of the natural man.

Literalism attempts to build a holy temple upon the sandy foundation of the religious self. It will suffer, sacrifice and labor, but it will not die. It is Adam at his pious best, but it has never denied self to take up the cross and follow Christ.

Prayer - Forgive me, Lord, for trying to follow You without taking up that self-death instrument daily."

Yet another way the depraved heart, cloaked fully in a mere form of religion, seeks to circumvent the work of the cross, is by denying or ignoring that there is a cross to take up **"daily."** The one whose theology is undergirded and poisoned with the unconditional eternal security lie, must resist all personal responsibility. He must take the line of least resistance. He is a moral coward, who while feigning to be walking in grace, has actually acquiesced to such a mythical position in order to avoid dying the death. He refuses to buy into the truth of the Gospel when it threatens his own personal comfort zone he has built around himself, using half truths and twisted and convoluted blends of philosophy, clichés, and Scripture. At all cost, he must remain intoxicated with the lie that he can do nothing to violate and fail the grace of God, and forfeit his place with God, which he erroneously believes is eternally secure –

no matter what rebellion he may choose to commit against Him who is "holy, holy, holy." (Isa. 6:3; Rev. 4:8) So, he must fight the truth violently using his keyboard, pulpit, or pen to defend his paper thin position. He must at all costs make sure anyone he leads believes that "God requires nothing of him, that salvation is of the LORD, and there is absolutely never any personal responsibility placed upon the individual recipient of salvation."

What a tragic, fraudulent lie this deceiver is casting upon those naïve enough to give him ear! The bowels of hell have been nourished by millions who have bought this lie, and have descended into the gaping and inescapable abyss (Isa. 5:14).

God forbid that anyone under the care of the "grace" deceiver be burdened with the slightest incentive or motivation to live holy, because in his evil theology, God Himself is no longer holy and just and doesn't punish sin in His own people. Using whatever deceptive means and even Scripture-twisting, the deceiver will do away with all thought of personal responsibility from among his flock. He further seeks to lull them asleep with himself, as they bask in the lukewarmness of hell-bound Laodicea and those **"at ease in Zion,"** refusing to hear and hearken to the severe warning to turn back to the LORD – **"Repent"** and **"Woe to them."** (Amos 6:1; Rev. 3:14-21)

Circumventing Schemes

In order to accomplish keeping his flock asleep, the beguiler must only acknowledge the *positional* cross, while seeking to deny the *experiential* or daily cross Christ commanded His followers to take up (Matt. 10:38-39; Mk. 8:34-39; Lk. 9:23-24). Those who deny the **"daily"** cross Christ commanded, deny Christ (Mk. 8:34-38). To deny His words is to deny Him (Mk. 8:38; Jn. 8:47; 14:21). Those who do not teach

Christ's command to deny self and take up the cross daily, hold a position of lawlessness; such are false teachers, **"ungodly men,"** who are **"turning the grace of our God into lasciviousness (a license for sin)."** (Rom. 6:1-2, 15; Jude 3-4) We are to **"earnestly contend"** against them and the heresies they spread.

Concerning the **"remnant,"** which is a descriptive word defining the only people to be eternally with Christ, Isaiah 37:31 says:

> **"And the remnant that is escaped of the house of Judah shall again take root downward, and bear fruit upward."**

No one can **"bear fruit upward"** unless he is willing to humble himself **"under the mighty hand of God."**

> **"Humble yourselves therefore under the mighty hand of God, that he may exalt you in due time:"** 1 Peter 5:6

The Last Days

God's Word forewarns us that only a few among those once made righteous will be in Heaven.

> **"And if the righteous scarcely be saved, where shall the ungodly and the sinner appear?"** 1 Peter 4:18

With all the popular last days type books in print, it is regrettable that few of them if any deal with readiness as the Scriptures present it. The human authors seem to completely overlook such an essential truth, because they have been schooled in this cross-denying way themselves. They completely overlook Christ's severe words of warning in Luke 21:34-36. The typical modern church posture is that if one has at some moment in the past received Christ, he is forever and indelibly secure for Heaven no matter what, with no possibility of losing out with God. Is this what the Bible teaches us?

Great tribulation is coming, such as has never been experienced upon the earth.

> **"For then shall be great tribulation, such as was not since the beginning of the world to this time, no, nor ever shall be." Matthew 24:21.**

We are told by the Son of God that only those with the oil of God in their vessels will be admitted into the marriage feast of the Lamb (Matt. 25:1-13). Only those who are intently connected with Jesus Christ, foregoing the things that would hinder their relationship with Him, will **"escape all these things that shall come to pass."**

> **"And take heed to yourselves, lest at any time your hearts be overcharged with surfeiting, and drunkenness, and cares of this life, and so that day come upon you unawares. For as a snare shall it come on all them that dwell on the face of the whole earth. Watch ye therefore, and pray always, that ye may be accounted worthy to escape all these things that shall come to pass, and to stand before the Son of man." Luke 21:34-36**

He told us that if we will overcome and be with Him, we must **"be accounted worthy to escape all these things that shall come to pass, and to stand before the Son of man."** By this we know that some shall not **"escape."**

The LORD Jesus beckoned those who would follow Him to the end, to be waiting and ready for His imminent and pending return:

> **"Let your loins be girded about, and your lights burning. And ye yourselves like unto men that wait for their lord, when he will return from the**

wedding; that when he cometh and knocketh, they may open unto him immediately. Blessed are those servants, whom the lord when he cometh shall find watching: verily I say unto you, that he shall gird himself, and make them to sit down to meat, and will come forth and serve them. And if he shall come in the second watch, or come in the third watch, and find them so, blessed are those servants. And this know, that if the goodman of the house had known what hour the thief would come, he would have watched, and not have suffered his house to be broken through. Be ye therefore ready also: for the Son of man cometh at an hour when ye think not." Luke 12:35-40

The enduring saints must discern keenly, and the only way to do such is to fully repent, love Him personally and supremely, and cast off all worldly ties that draw us from the Bridegroom (Rev. 3:14-18).

In order to escape this promised and epidemic onslaught of the enemy of God, one must be daily **"crucified with Christ,"** being separate from iniquity and abiding in Christ (Jn. 15:1-6; Gal. 2:20). It is only in being **"dead"** that we are **"hid with Christ in God."** (Col. 3:3) It is only in experiencing His **"death"** that His **"life"** can work in us and through us to others (2 Cor. 4:10-12). It is only in taking **"root downward"** that He will raise us up to **"bear fruit upward."** (Isa. 37:31)

As was prophesied, the enemy's seduction of souls is in full swing and ever-increasing as the time of the return of Jesus draws nigh:

"Therefore rejoice, ye heavens, and ye that dwell in them. Woe to the inhabiters of the earth and of the sea! for the devil is come down unto you, having

great wrath, because he knoweth that he hath but a short time." Revelation 12:12

In the above passage, those who are already safe with Him in Heaven are told to **"rejoice,"** while those who remain upon the earth in this last hour are solemnly warned to beware because **"the devil is come down unto you, having great wrath, because he knoweth that he hath but a short time."**

Perhaps there would yet remain among us some who are still ignorant of the devices of the enemy, and not so sure about the activities he is perpetrating among the remnant. Listen closely to 1 John 2:26-3:3, which states:

"These things have I written unto you concerning them that seduce you (this is John's inspired reason for writing to us). But the anointing which ye have received of him abideth (remains) in you, and ye need not that any man teach you: but as the same anointing teacheth you of all things, and is truth, and is no lie, and even as it hath taught you, ye shall abide in him. And now, little children, abide (remain) in him; that, when he shall appear, we may have confidence, and not be ashamed before him at his coming. If ye know that he is righteous, ye know that every one that doeth righteousness is born of him. Behold, what manner of love the Father hath bestowed upon us, that we should be called the sons of God: therefore the world knoweth us not, because it knew him not. Beloved, now are we the sons of God, and it doth not yet appear what we shall be: but we know that, when he shall appear, we shall be like him; for we shall see him as he is. And every man that hath this hope in him (the hope of Christ's soon return) purifieth himself, even as he is pure."

According to these Holy Spirit inspired words penned by John the apostle, there are **"many deceivers"** seeking to **"seduce you."** (1 Jn. 2:26; 2 Jn. 7-11) One of the most insidious ways these wolves, who **"lie in wait to deceive,"** operate, is by refraining from preaching the true Gospel which includes the taking up of the daily cross (Matt. 16:24-27; Lk. 9:23-24). If one will be safe in heavenly glory, never to suffer another iota of pain for all the eternal future, he must stay clear of the **"many deceivers"** who have answered the call of evil, and are sent forth to **"deceive"** those who would be prey due to:

- Having a lack of knowledge – not knowing the Scriptures nor the power of God (Hos. 4:6; Matt. 22:29)

- Not watching and praying (Matt. 26:41)

- Not submitting to God (James 4:7)

- Not being crucified with Christ (Gal. 2:20)

- Not being **"dead"** and having their lives **"hid with Christ in God."** (Col. 3:3)

- Not having their affections set upon things above (Col. 3:1-4)

- Minding earthly things (Phil. 3:18-19)

There is abundant proof that so many today vainly believe they can have the benefits of the cross without the responsibility of the cross. They want the crown but not the cross. They are self-serving (**"whose god is their belly"**), and so desire to feel secure by trusting that because Christ died and was buried and rose again, they are safe.

As was long ago foretold, many in this deceived generation are trusting in Christ's atoning death without their own personal participation. They call Him **"Lord, Lord,"** but in the end will hear the horrific words of termination, **"Depart from me."** (Matt. 7:21-23) From His blessed presence they will be forever alienated, vanquished into **"the lake of fire."** (Rev. 20:11-15)

> **"Not every one that saith unto me, Lord, Lord, shall enter into the kingdom of heaven; but he that doeth the will of my Father which is in heaven. Many will say to me in that day, Lord, Lord, have we not prophesied in thy name? and in thy name have cast out devils? and in thy name done many wonderful works? And then will I profess unto them, I never knew you: depart from me, ye that work iniquity (lawlessness)." Matthew 7:21-23**

So many who claim the name of Christ conveniently ignore what Jesus said about taking up the cross and following Him to the end. In the riveting words listed in the above passage, did not Jesus tell us that only **"he that doeth the will of my Father which is in heaven"** will be allowed in His Heaven?

According to the Son of God, overcomers will be allowed into Heaven and no one else (Rev. 2-3).

Readiness test:

- Are you daily taking up your cross? (Matt. 16:24-25)

- Do you daily deny yourself so that Christ can reign in your mortal body? (Lk. 9:23-24; 2 Cor. 4:11-12)

- Are you following Christ in the way He prescribed? (Matt. 7:21; Jn. 8:47; 1 Jn. 2:3-6)

- Are you purifying your life of all that offends God? (Acts 15:9; 2 Cor. 7:1; 1 Jn. 3:3)

- Are you coming out from this sinful world system and the apostate religious system? (2 Cor. 6:14-7:1; 1 Jn. 2:14-17)

- In obedience to the LORD, are you remaining clear of any and all wolves, who preach or pen a cross-less gospel? (2 Cor. 11:2-5; Phil. 3:18-19)

- Are you learning yet more and more to hate this sinful and rebellious world system, lest you become the enemy of God? (James 4:4; 1 Jn. 2:15-17)

- Are you daily in the Word so the Word is getting into you and washing your heart and mind of all that is not according to the mind of Christ? (Ps. 119:9, 11; Prov. 4:4, 21; Jer. 15:16; Jn. 15:3; Eph. 5:26)

- Are you keeping your lamp full by daily communion with Jesus? (Matt. 25:1-13; 1 Jn. 1:3-9)

- Are you abstaining from fleshly lusts and departing from all iniquity? (2 Tim. 2:19; 1 Pet. 2:11)

- Are you overcoming the wiles of the enemy who seeks to seduce you from self-denial? (1 Jn. 2:26-3:3)

- Are you watching and praying, so as to be blessed to take up your cross daily and not be seduced from essential obedience in following Christ? (Matt. 26:41; Lk. 12:35-40)

- Are you watching and praying so as to escape all sin and remain ever-ready for Christ's soon appearing? (Prov. 8:34; Matt. 26:41; Lk. 21:34-36)

- Are you calling others to come to the Fountain of living waters from which all life flows, and in which all blessings abide? (Rev. 22:17)

In this late hour, may God bless each of us - His children - to be in fellowship with those who are embracing instead of evading the daily cross, and who **"call on the Lord out of a pure heart."** (2 Tim. 2:22)

As we were long ago forewarned, the **"great wrath"** of the one who **"knoweth that he hath but a short (brief) time"** has **"come down"** upon us through an epidemic of apostate leaders, who like the deceivers of old, erroneously promise His eternal life to those who refuse to take up their crosses to follow Him (Jer. 23:17; Amos 9:10; 2 Pet. 2; Jude 3-4). Beware!

> **"Beware lest any man spoil you through philosophy and vain deceit, after the tradition of men, after the rudiments of the world, and not after Christ." Colossians 2:8**

PRAYER: *Jesus, please deeply quicken Your holy fear in my inner most being. From this instant forward, I look fervently for Your soon return. Heavenly Father, I beg You to unite my heart to fear Thy name and make ultra sensitive my conscience – to be so easily convicted upon the slightest thought that varies from Your holy will. Into Your hands, I now commend my spirit. Amen.*

Capture Points

1. Read and discuss Matthew 27:43 and how it applied to Christ when He was on the cross, and how this same temptation applies to the believer in his daily walk with Jesus.

2. Transcribe 1 Peter 4:18 on an index card and discuss. (KJV recommended)

3. Read and discuss Luke 12:35-40. (KJV recommended)

Chapter Eleven

The Intentional Circumvention of the Cross

"As many as desire to make a fair shew in the flesh, they constrain you to be circumcised; only lest they should suffer persecution for the cross of Christ. For neither they themselves who are circumcised keep the law; but desire to have you circumcised, that they may glory in your flesh. But God forbid that I should glory, save in the cross of our Lord Jesus Christ, by whom the world is crucified unto me, and I unto the world." Galatians 6:12-14

Circumventing the cross is a deadly undertaking and has eternal consequences attached to it. Peter temporarily played the wolf when he sought to circumvent Christ's going to the cross:

"From that time forth began Jesus to shew unto his disciples, how that he must go unto Jerusalem, and suffer many things of the elders and chief priests and scribes, and be killed, and be raised again the third day. Then Peter took him, and began to rebuke him, saying, Be it far from thee, Lord: this shall not

> be unto thee. But he turned, and said unto Peter, Get thee behind me, Satan: thou art an offence unto me: for thou savourest not the things that be of God, but those that be of men. Then said Jesus unto his disciples, If any *man* will come after me, let him deny himself, and take up his cross, and follow me. For whosoever will save his life shall lose it: and whosoever will lose his life for my sake shall find it. For what is a man profited, if he shall gain the whole world, and lose his own soul? or what shall a man give in exchange for his soul?" Matthew 16:21-26

"Satan" was seeking to hinder God's plan of redemption using Peter – one of Christ's own – to circumvent the redeeming cross. In the same way, today "Satan" seeks to circumvent the truth of the cross in order to hinder men from being free from him, sin, and the world. "Satan" cannot change the accomplished fact of the redemption of Christ on the cross – "It is finished." (Jn. 19:30) In spite of this, what he has been very successful at doing is installing a priesthood of cross-less wolves who deny Christ while pretending to be representing Him. Their message is different than His and they are thereby concluded to be antichrist. Any person sitting under the teaching of a leader who is not preaching the cross of Jesus should immediately flee for his life. That pastor or author has counted **"the preaching of the cross"** as **"foolishness,"** and by such identifies himself as one who is **"perishing."** (1 Cor. 1:18) Such a man is circumventing the work of the cross.

First off, is Satan active and scheming in his desire to steal, kill, and destroy? (Jn. 10:10; 1 Pet. 5:8) Well, look at how he worked in Peter in the passage above – to get rid of the cross experience. Does he have an organized plan? Yes (2 Cor. 2:11).

Let's peer into yet another instance where our LORD Jesus was given opportunity to dodge going to or through the cross for the sins of the world – the very reason for which He came (1 Tim. 1:15). The setting is the garden of Gethsemane, where Judas and his band of men entered looking for Christ.

> **"Judas then, having received a band of men and officers from the chief priests and Pharisees, cometh thither with lanterns and torches and weapons. Jesus therefore, knowing all things that should come upon him, went forth, and said unto them, Whom seek ye?" John 18:3-4**

When asked, Jesus openly identified Himself. He hid nothing. The story continues ...

> **"Then Simon Peter having a sword drew it, and smote the high priest's servant, and cut off his right ear. The servant's name was Malchus. Then said Jesus unto Peter, Put up thy sword into the sheath: the cup which my Father hath given me, shall I not drink it?" John 18:10-11**

In his zeal, Peter took to the flesh to protect Christ. Although Christ had told him often that His mission included suffering and death, he still did not realize that it was for this very cross his LORD had come into the world. Jesus again rebuked Peter for seeking to circumvent His heavenly mission to die. The turning away of Christ from the shedding of His blood for the sins of the world, would have derailed the plan of God to buy back a people for Himself (Matt. 26:28; Acts 20:28). Jesus could never have risen again on the third day had He not first died on that wooden cross (Rom. 4:25).

Question: Why would sinful self and Satan desire to stop the work of the cross in the life of Christ's disciples?

Answer: When Christians are drawn by the gravitational pull of evil and the influence of the enemy – away from the cross that sentences the carnal man to death, they instead go the way of **"the works of the flesh,"** which are soul-damning sins, and they are unfruitful in walking pleasing to the LORD and winning others to Christ (Gal. 5:19-21).

Outside of a crucifixion of the old man or the sinful nature, made possible by the Holy Spirit, the individual also:

- Does not intimately come to know the Father and Son (Jn. 17:3; Phil. 3:7-10; 1 Jn. 1:3, 7).

- Inevitably lives in sin (Rom. 6).

- Does not become **"Rooted and built up in him, and stablished in the faith, as ye have been taught, abounding therein with thanksgiving."** (Col. 2:6-7)

- Does not become of an **"honest and good heart ... and bring forth fruit with patience."** (Lk. 8:15)

- Is disobedient to the Great Commission by neglecting to seek out lost souls (Mk. 16:15).

Satan does not want havoc wreaked upon his dark kingdom by Holy Ghost filled, crucified believers. He has so many souls under the dark shadow of his fear and deceit, and the LORD uses His people to break through that bondage with His Word (2 Cor. 4:4-7). When this happens, **"the world"** is turned **"upside down,"** which means men and women are convicted and brought to repentance and salvation in Christ (Acts 17:6; 20:21).

> **"(Jesus came) To open their eyes, and to turn them from darkness to light, and from the power of Satan unto God, that they may receive forgiveness of sins, and inheritance among them which are sanctified by faith that is in me." Acts 26:18**

The way Christ delivers us from His and our enemy, is by the blood of His cross and the daily cross which keeps us separate from the flesh, world, and devil. Speaking of the call of the enemy to get us off of the cross – circumvention, Travis Bryan III writes:

> "Any day I'm dying, there is a spontaneous resurrecting. Our part is to get down or sink down. Resurrection is automatic. Life always, and only, springs out of death. Today is for the most part a resurrection day because I have allowed the Lord to keep me on the cross so far. The devil is always beckoning us, like the mockers did Jesus, to 'come down from the cross. Save yourself .....'"

When we come down off the cross, we become fruitless, non-productive for Christ, and as salt that has lost its flavor and is **"good for nothing, but to be cast out, and to be trodden under foot of men."** (Matt. 5:13)

The Cross-Less Gospel of the Modern Church

The landscape of American churches is filled with a cross-less gospel which is no gospel at all. Self-serving hirelings fill most pulpits, media spotlights, and positions of influence over millions who claim to be following Christ, and they have perpetrated upon these masses a false gospel full of **"damnable heresies."** (2 Pet. 2:1)

Regrettably, the message and methods of the modern church world are utterly not according to the biblical pattern – they are corrupt, and leading millions to the worship of self as was foretold concerning the final days of this age (Isa. 9:16; 1 Tim. 4:1-3; 2 Tim. 3:1-7; 4:3-4). This cross-less gospel is a false gospel. It is **"another gospel"** and will ultimately result in the damnation of millions (2 Cor. 11:4; Gal. 1:6-10). Jesus is calling all who will be with Him eternally to repent – to return fully to Him – and hear what He is saying to the Church in this last hour. **"He that hath an ear, let him hear what the Spirit saith unto the churches; To him that overcometh will I give to eat of the tree of life, which is in the midst of the paradise of God."** (Rev. 2:7)

The person who is possessed by a self-serving "What's in it for ME" mentality instead of "How can I most please my LORD Jesus," is going to discover just how Luciferic his current views are. It is prayerfully hoped that he will be brought to repentance *now*, and a laying down of his life, that Christ alone might reign in him (Isa. 14:12-15; James 4:6-10). Ready or not – Jesus is coming (Lk. 21:34-36). Are you ready?

If a person will not die to sin and self, he might as well stop pretending to be a Christian. Such a person has a deeper love for self than Jesus Christ, and possesses only **"a form of godliness, but denying the power"** or authority of Christ to reign in his life (2 Tim. 3:5).

To **"die daily"** is to love and prefer Christ above ourselves by allowing the blessed work of crucifixion to transpire, and to refuse to allow the circumventing of the cross and its work in us.

> "Self-denial is indispensable if God's redeeming love is to display power and blessing in my life." Andrew Murray

As was the case of Peter when he sought to stop Christ from doing the Father's will by going to the cross, so **"Satan"** is behind any attempt to circumvent the work of the cross in the lives of believers (Matt. 16:23). There are **"seducing spirits and doctrines of devils"** which work through false leaders and systems of religion to entice the believer to indulge in the lusts of the flesh and **"mind earthly things."** (Phil. 3:17-19; 1 Tim. 4:1)

> **"Now the Spirit speaketh expressly, that in the latter times some shall depart from the faith, giving heed to seducing spirits, and doctrines of devils."**
> **1 Timothy 4:1**

After the myriad of warnings given to us by Christ and His apostles, should we be shocked at the percentage of hireling wolves operating in the church world and media today? No honest and avid Bible student is shocked. He is rather seeing the Scriptures he loves coming to pass before his very eyes, as **"many"** are being **"led away with the error of the wicked"** by the **"many false prophets."** (Matt. 7:15; 24:4-5, 11, 24; 2 Pet. 3:17; 1 Jn. 4:1)

As so many today are discovering and enacting in their personal lives, it is much better to **"flee the wrath to come"** by getting out of the modern church world and all of its placebo "worship," than to stay among them.

> **"For the congregation of hypocrites shall be desolate, and fire shall consume the tabernacles of bribery." Job 15:34**

> **"I have hated the congregation of evil doers; and will not sit with the wicked." Psalms 26:5**

I love the biblical phrase, **"the simplicity that is in Christ."** (2 Cor. 11:3)

In this passage of Scripture, Paul reveals his **"fear"** for Christians, and in particular the believers in Corinth. This is seen in verses 2-4 when he says, **"For I am jealous over you with godly jealousy: for I have espoused you to one husband, that I may present you as a chaste virgin to Christ. But <u>I fear, lest by any means, as the serpent beguiled Eve through his subtilty, so your minds should be corrupted from the simplicity that is in Christ</u>. For if he that cometh preacheth <u>another Jesus</u>, whom we have not preached, or** if ye receive <u>another spirit</u>, which ye have not received, or <u>another gospel</u>, which ye have not accepted, ye might well bear with him." The apostle Paul is warning Christ's disciples of all historic ages here. He was in **"fear"** that these believers would **"bear with (allow)"** those **"false apostles"** who were posing as Christ's messengers. He feared that they would **"beguile"** these Christians by moving them away from the **"simplicity (singleness, sincerity) that is in Christ"** to **"another Jesus … another spirit … another gospel."** (2 Cor. 11:2-5; 12-15)

Isn't this what so many leaders are doing today? Have they not, with **"<u>subtilty</u>,"** misguided people away from the cross? Have they not, by their purposeful neglect, replaced **"the preaching of the cross"** with human philosophies, programs, books by famous human authors who are deceivers, self-pleasing psychology, 12-step programs, and entertainment? (1 Cor. 1:18)

> **"The ear that heareth the reproof of life abideth among the wise." Proverbs 15:31**

Abiding or remaining **"among the wise"** requires breaking fellowship with such **"enemies of the cross of Christ,"** who **"mind earthly things"** while rejecting the heavenly things Christ and His apostles gave us in the Holy Scriptures (2 Tim. 3:16-4:5).

The true disciple should at once depart from such heretics who circumvent the cross and its work by not preaching it (Prov. 19:27). Please remember the words of the prophet Isaiah as the Holy Spirit moved upon him to write:

> **"Bind up the testimony, seal the law among my disciples … To the law and to the testimony: if they speak not according to this word, it is because there is no light in them." Isaiah 8:16, 20**

Did you catch the truth here? Where He told us that if someone does not speak according to His Word/law, it reveals that such a person has no light from the LORD in himself? According to this truth, any and every time we listen to someone speak, we should stand back and ask ourselves whether or not this person is speaking according to the Holy Scriptures (of course, contextually). See Acts 17:11 and 2 Timothy 2:15.

This writer has personally experienced great and blessed freedom by coming out from among the false churches that are so plentiful in our land, and which misrepresent Christ grossly.

Where is the cross in the modern church world? Have we been cheated, and thereby misled and deceived?

Remnant believers are to come out from among the wicked, who have a mere **"form of godliness"** and **"deny"** the rule of Jesus in their personal lives (2 Tim. 3:1-7). We should not continue to dwell among those who give ear to a cross-less gospel (2 Cor. 6:14-7:1; Rev. 18:4).

The message of the cross has been so under-preached that when speaking about it to individuals and groups, one can observe a dumbfounded state in the eyes of those listening. It's like they have never heard this message spoken to them. However, many of those who read their Bibles are at least somewhat familiar with the myriad of Scriptures on this important topic. So, let's be diligent to plant the seed of God's Word – the seed of the cross – into the hearts of men, and God will do the rest (Isa. 55:11; 1 Cor. 1:18; 3:6-9).

The Importance of the Cross

Only Christ can solve the problem of sin. Only Christ can subdue the sinful nature in us, by our obedient application of the cross He told us to **"take up."** (Matt. 16:24-25)

When speaking to the Corinthian church, in the very midst of addressing carnality, idolatry, and immaturity, Paul spoke of **"the preaching of the cross."** (1 Cor. 1:18) The cross is God's answer to our ailments and must be declared as the solution of the LORD to these, and a myriad of other, otherwise unsolvable problems.

> "The cross is the key to all situations as well as to all Scripture." L. E. Maxwell

The cross was the implement of death by which Jesus Christ was going to pay the price for the sins of the whole world. That is why He came to the earth (Matt. 26:28; Jn. 1:29; 1 Tim. 1:15; Rev. 1:5; 13:8). The cross is the implement of death to the self-life in the daily walk of the true disciple. We know, from the above passage and others, that any leader who seeks to circumvent or underplay (play down by not preaching) the place of the cross in the life of the individual believer, is a **"deceitful worker"** and one of Satan's **"ministers."** (2 Cor. 11:12-15) Where there is no cross preached, there is no death to that which God told us is at enmity with Him.

> **"Because the carnal mind *is* enmity against God: for it is not subject to the law of God, neither indeed can be. So then they that are in the flesh cannot please God." Romans 8:7-8**

The resurrection life of Christ will not occur in any life that is not first laid down. Without death to self, there can be no life of Christ manifested. Here's how it all works:

> **"Always bearing about in the body the dying of the Lord Jesus, that the life also of Jesus might be made manifest in our body. For we which live are always delivered unto death for Jesus' sake, that the life also of Jesus might be made manifest in our mortal flesh." 2 Corinthians 4:10-11**

Are you beginning to see the danger and travesty of circumventing the cross? It's only as we take up the cross daily and are crucified with Jesus, that His life will work in us to His glory.

To deny the daily cross is to deny Christ, who stated the following:

> **"And when he had called the people unto him with his disciples also, he said unto them, Whosoever will come after me, let him deny himself, and take up his cross, and follow me ... Whosoever therefore shall be ashamed of <u>me AND of my words</u> in this adulterous and sinful generation; of him also shall the Son of man be ashamed, when he cometh in the glory of his Father with the holy angels." Mark 8:34, 38**

> **"And he said to them all, If any man will come after me, let him deny himself, and take up his cross daily, and follow me. For whosoever will save his life shall lose it: but whosoever will lose his life for my sake, the same shall save it." Luke 9:23-24**

The modern gospel itself is a replacement for the old rugged cross preached widely in previous generations. The new cross is no cross at all, and comes with another gospel that is not the true Gospel Christ preached. This modern gospel circumvents the cross. In these following words, A.W. Tozer captures the difference between the original Gospel of the cross and the new one that is rampant in this last hour:

> "The Old Cross and the New
>
> Unannounced and mostly undetected there has come in modern times a new cross into popular evangelical circles. It is like the old cross, but different:

the likenesses are superficial; the differences, fundamental.

From this new cross has sprung a new philosophy of the Christian life, and from that new philosophy has come a new evangelical technique - a new type of meeting and a new kind of preaching. This new evangelism employs the same language as the old, but its content is not the same and its emphasis not as before.

The old cross would have no truck with the world. For Adam's proud flesh it meant the end of the journey. It carried into effect the sentence imposed by the law of Sinai. The new cross is not opposed to the human race; rather, it is a friendly pal and, if understood aright, it is the source of oceans of good clean fun and innocent enjoyment. It lets Adam live without interference. His life motivation is unchanged; he still lives for his own pleasure, only now he takes delight in singing choruses and watching religious movies instead of singing bawdy songs and drinking hard liquor. The accent is still on enjoyment, though the fun is now on a higher plane morally if not intellectually.

The new cross encourages a new and entirely different evangelistic approach. The evangelist does not demand abnegation of the old life before a new life can be received. He preaches not contrasts but similarities. He seeks to key into public interest by showing that Christianity makes no unpleasant demands; rather, it offers the same thing the world does, only on a higher level. Whatever the sin-mad world happens to be clamoring after at the moment is cleverly shown to be the very thing the gospel offers, only the religious product is better.

The new cross does not slay the sinner, it redirects him. It gears him into a cleaner and jollier way of living and saves his self-respect. To the self-assertive it says, 'Come and assert yourself for Christ.' To the egotist it says, 'Come and do your boasting in the Lord.' To the thrill-seeker it says, 'Come and enjoy the thrill of Christian fellowship.' The Christian message is slanted in the direction of the current vogue in order to make it acceptable to the public.

The philosophy back of this kind of thing may be sincere but its sincerity does not save it from being false. It is false because it is blind. It misses completely the whole meaning of the cross.

The old cross is a symbol of death. It stands for the abrupt, violent end of a human being. The man in Roman times who took up his cross and started down the road had already said good-by to his friends. He was not coming back. He was going out to have it ended. The cross made no compromise, modified nothing, spared nothing; it slew all of the man, completely and for good. It did not try to keep on good terms with its victim. It struck cruel and hard, and when it had finished its work, the man was no more.

The race of Adam is under death sentence. There is no commutation and no escape. God cannot approve any of the fruits of sin, however innocent they may appear or beautiful to the eyes of men. God salvages the individual by liquidating him and then raising him again to newness of life.

That evangelism which draws friendly parallels between the ways of God and the ways of men is false to the Bible and cruel to the souls of its hearers.

173

The faith of Christ does not parallel the world, it intersects it. In coming to Christ we do not bring our old life up onto a higher plane; we leave it at the cross. The corn of wheat must fall into the ground and die.

We who preach the gospel must not think of ourselves as public relations agents sent to establish good will between Christ and the world. We must not imagine ourselves commissioned to make Christ acceptable to big business, the press, the world of sports or modern education. We are not diplomats but prophets, and our message is not a compromise but an ultimatum.

God offers life, but not an improved old life. The life He offers is life out of death. It stands always on the far side of the cross. Whoever would possess it must pass under the rod. He must repudiate himself and concur in God's just sentence against him. What does this mean to the individual, the condemned man who would find life in Christ Jesus? How can this theology be translated into life? Simply, he must repent and believe. He must forsake his sins and then go on to forsake himself. Let him cover nothing, defend nothing, excuse nothing. Let him not seek to make terms with God, but let him bow his head before the stroke of God's stern displeasure and acknowledge himself worthy to die.

Having done this let him gaze with simple trust upon the risen Saviour, and from Him will come life and rebirth and cleansing and power. The cross that ended the earthly life of Jesus now puts an end to the sinner; and the power that raised Christ from the dead now raises him to a new life along with Christ....

Dare we, the heirs of such a legacy of power, tamper with the truth? Dare we... alter the pattern shown us in the Mount? May God forbid. Let us preach the old cross and we will know the old power."

PRAYER: *LORD, forgive me for self idolatry and spiritual adultery in not looking fully and with open face to Thee. I want to be lost in You, Jesus – to lose my life in You that I might gain it. Forgive me for buying into a false gospel that is not Yours, and please open my eyes to distinguish between the new gospel and the true Gospel and the message of the cross. I love You, Jesus, and am joyfully crucified with You.*

Todd Tomasella

Capture Points

1. Write out on an index card 1 Corinthians 1:18 and discuss (KJV recommended).

2. Discuss Isaiah 8:16, 20.

3. Discuss and meditate upon Mark 8:34, 38.

Chapter Twelve

The Conquering & Victorious Power of Desire

"Through desire a man, having separated himself, seeketh and intermeddleth with all wisdom."
Proverbs 18:1

What causes someone to seek and intermeddle with wisdom? **"Desire."** It's **"Through desire"** that a person sets aside all else in order to pursue and master the desired object or subject. He sets himself apart to learn that matter, diligently studying everything he can concerning it. In the case of the kingdom of the LORD, the genuine disciple distinguishes himself as such by putting aside all that does not lead him closer to the Savior.

> **"If any *man* come to me, and hate not (love less than Christ) his father, and mother, and wife, and children, and brethren, and sisters, yea, and his own life also, he cannot be my disciple. And whosoever doth not bear his cross, and come after me, cannot be my disciple." Luke 14:26-27**

I must ask: Who is it that I love? Who fills my heart? Who is it that my heart affections are set upon? Whose existence and life fills my thoughts with delight?

To further illustrate this point, allow me to attempt painting a picture using something we all understand about the love between a man and a woman. Men, do you remember somewhere in your past how that although *Sue* might have wanted to spend time with you, you seemed too busy with too many things and unable to spend but small portions of time here and there with her? Yet, when *Mary* came along, all of a sudden you found volumes of time to spend with her because you were enamored with her. In fact, you couldn't stay away from her. Both of you were enraptured with one another and because of this you suddenly found creative ways to adjust your previously "unalterable" and "too busy" routine. Your previously rigid schedule suddenly possessed the ability to be manipulated and so you made time effortlessly to spend with *Mary*. Why? Because you desired her. Your heart leapt at the thought of her. Butterflies fluttered in your bosom as you picked up the phone to call her or drove to meet her for dinner – *because she was your desire*. You were consumed with her and so there was little that you wouldn't do to clear the way to be with her, to cherish her, to love her more.

Isn't this how we are when Christ is truly our **"first love"**? (Rev. 2:4-5)

> **"Delight thyself also in the LORD ..." Psalms 37:4**
>
> **"Thy testimonies (words) also are my delight and my counsellors." Psalms 119:24**
>
> **"I have longed for thy salvation, O LORD; and thy law (Word) is my delight." Psalms 119:174**

"One *thing* have I desired of the LORD, that will I seek after; that I may dwell in the house of the LORD all the days of my life, to behold the beauty of the LORD, and to inquire in his temple." Psalms 27:4

"As the hart panteth after the water brooks, so panteth my soul after thee, O God. My soul thirsteth for God, for the living God: when shall I come and appear before God?" Psalms 42:1-2

David was the only man called by God **"a man after mine own heart, which shall fulfil all my will."** (Acts 13:22) Those who choose to pant, hunger, and thirst after more and more of Christ, delight to deny themselves and decrease, that He might increase (Matt. 5:6; Lk. 9:23-24; Jn. 3:30). These are His true remnant, and unrelentingly seek His face as they freely choose to **"take root downward, and bear fruit upward."** (1 Chron. 22:19; Isa. 37:31).

1 Peter 2:2 says, **"As newborn babes, <u>desire</u> the sincere (pure) milk of the word, that ye may grow thereby."** Here the LORD tells us what to **"desire,"** and that is **"the sincere milk of the word"** of God. By the simple fact that He told us specifically what to **"desire,"** we know that *desire* is driven by the will of the individual. Desire is a choice. Desiring God and His Word go together. Desiring or longing for more of Him is the heartbeat of those who truly know Him (Ps. 27:4, 8; Jn. 17:3; Phil. 3:10).

Desire is fed by the choice of our activities. Choosing to dwell in intimate, unbroken fellowship with the Savior stirs in us a deep desire to know Him more and to obey Him daily and moment by moment. The desire to know Him – the very reason for which we have been created—will drive us to set ourselves apart to read, study, memorize, and meditate upon what He gave us in His Word, and to dwell with Him in daily prayer communion.

> **"Through desire a man, having separated himself, seeketh and intermeddleth with all wisdom."**
> **Proverbs 18:1**

Desire Drives Our Behavior

Why do some people who are Christians have such an aptitude to know all the quarterbacks, running backs, and players in the NFL? It's simple – they have chosen to desire and therefore spend time watching, reading, studying, and learning about these teams and players. There is no inference here that sports in themselves are sinful. Yet, Christ did warn us concerning lusting after (unduly desiring) other things, even those not sinful in themselves, and placing them before our love for Him:

> **"And have no root in themselves, and so endure but for a time: afterward, when affliction or persecution ariseth for the word's sake, immediately they are offended. And these are they which are sown among thorns; such as hear the word, And <u>the cares of this world</u>, and <u>the deceitfulness of riches</u>, and <u>the lusts of other things</u> entering in, choke the word, and it becometh unfruitful." Mark 4:17-19**

Those who **"have no root in themselves"** have not chosen to delight themselves in the LORD and are therefore not sinking down deep into the death of Christ. They are therefore shallow rooted, and if repentance is not rendered, will be eventually uprooted (Mk. 4:17; Jude 12). Those who do not obey Christ by laying aside their self-will and self-ambition will inevitably be drawn away into **"the cares of this world,"** and His Word will become **"unfruitful"** in them.

Why do some ladies among us seem so drawn to learn all the latest romance "secrets" that entice them on the flashy covers of modern day magazines? Why do they buy those paper rags and drink in the world's notions of a perverted "love"? Then, some turn around and say "I just don't seem to have the ability to memorize God's Word." Is that true? Why are they **"dull of hearing"?** (Heb. 5:11) Why do they not have ears to hear **"what the Spirit saith unto the churches"?** (Rev. 2:7) Could it be that their desire is not pointed at Jesus? Could it be that the affections of their hearts are on self and this fleeting world? Do they not have the ability to learn and memorize? Of course they do! Yet, due to not choosing to *desire* the Person of Christ and His Word, they are dull of hearing and unable to absorb His truth (Jn. 8:31-32; 47; 17:17; 2 Tim. 3:7). Do those men who know and understand their favorite sport not also have the aptitude to learn and memorize the divine Precepts? Well, it's obvious that we all have been gifted with the ability to know, understand, and memorize many things – and yet we have memorized what we have desired.

> **"The counsel of the LORD standeth for ever, the thoughts of his heart to all generations." Psalms 33:11**

The LORD told us that He has given to us in His written Counsel (Word) the very **"thoughts of his heart."** (Ps. 33:11) Those who love Him desire to know **"the thoughts of his heart."**

> **"One thing have I desired of the LORD, that will I seek after; that I may dwell in the house of the LORD all the days of my life, to behold the beauty of the LORD, and to enquire in his temple." Psalms 27:4**

The **"man after God's own heart"** had **"One"** consuming **"thing"** that he **"desired,"** and that was to **"behold the beauty of the LORD."** (Ps. 27:4; Acts 13:22) If He is my *delight* – if I am delighting in Him – His Word becomes my all-consuming delight. The two cannot be separated. He is the living Word, revealed by the Holy Spirit through His written Word.

The person who desires the LORD more than his own self and way, will lay all down for the blessed privilege of Christ reigning in his life. It's all about who one loves most – self or the Savior (Rom. 6:16).

Jeremiah the prophet delighted in the LORD and therefore in His words:

> **"Thy words were found, and I did eat them; and thy word was unto me the joy and rejoicing of mine heart: for I am called by thy name, O LORD God of hosts." Jeremiah 15:16**

May God bless us to be quickened in this late hour – to be united in our hearts to fear His holy name and to seek His face continually. Amen.

PRAYER: *Heavenly Father, I acknowledge my sins of idolatry and spiritual adultery before You. I have placed other gods (idols) before Thee and now turn back to You in repentance. Please forgive my many sins and grant Your holy grace to my heart to change me forever. I love You, Jesus – there is none beside Thee, LORD Jesus. From this moment forward I choose to delight in You as my very first love. Amen.*

Capture Points

1. Talk about the 3 things which Jesus tells us **"choke the word,"** as is recorded in Mark 4:17-19.

2. Write out Psalms 33:11 on an index card (KJV recommended).

3. Discuss and mediate upon Jeremiah 15:16.

Chapter Thirteen

"I Keep Under My Body"
1 Corinthians 9:27

"But <u>I keep under (subdue) my body, and bring</u> *it*
<u>into subjection</u>: lest that by any means, when I have
preached to others, I myself should be a castaway."
1 Corinthians 9:27

When he said the words **"I die daily,"** the apostle Paul was
speaking of daily laying aside his own personal will that
Christ might reign in his mortal body, and that he might
be ever prepared to meet the LORD and to be resurrected
to life everlasting (Lk. 4:14; 22:42; Jn. 5:28-29; 1 Cor. 15:31;
2 Cor. 4:10-11; 1 Thess. 4:16-18). These words of Paul are
hemmed up against the next chapter, and the ensuing
words – chapter 10:1-12 – make it abundantly clear that the
decision to follow Christ just the way He prescribed, is all
important to our eternal destiny. In this passage the Holy
Spirit inspired the apostle to cite five specific sins that reveal
self-love in lieu of love for Christ, and how such disqualifies
one from the ultimate prize.

Contrary to much false teaching today, this apostle of
grace did not believe that he was unconditionally eternally

secure. He fully believed that the potential of falling away and becoming a **"castaway"** existed (1 Cor. 9:27). It was a concern of his, both for himself and for those he taught. Becoming a **"castaway"** simply means being *cast away* from the LORD in the end. The end of all those who leave the earth in Christ – dead to self and alive in Him – is that they will forever be with Him.

> **"But <u>I keep under (subdue) my body, and bring</u> *<u>it</u>* <u>into subjection</u>: lest that by any means, when I have preached to others, I myself should be a castaway."** **1 Corinthians 9:27**

If one is going to be a true Bible believer, he must acknowledge that the saint *can* forfeit his place with the LORD if he neglects, casts away, falls away from, or departs from saving faith in Jesus (Ezek. 33:12-13; Matt. 10:22; 25:10-13; Lk. 8:13; 1 Tim. 4:1; 5:12; Heb. 3:6, 12-15; 10:26-39). In order to avoid falling away, one must **"mortify the deeds of the body,"** and continue to live in and be led by the Holy Spirit (Rom. 8:13-14). Those who deny Christ instead of self will be denied by Him (2 Tim. 2:12). Many want to "feel" secure, and so much teaching today accommodates their desire; yet, the Word of God is void of any promise of eternal security to any person who is not presently abiding in Christ (Jn. 15:1-6; Rev. 22:11). Eternal life is offered exclusively to those who love Him enough to **"suffer with him."** (Rom. 8:17; 2 Tim. 2:11-12)

> **"And if children, then heirs; heirs of God, and joint-heirs with Christ; <u>if so be that we suffer with</u> *<u>him</u>*<u>, that we may be also glorified together</u>. For I reckon that the sufferings of this present time *are* not worthy *to be compared* with the glory which shall be revealed in us." Romans 8:17-18**

Any posture conveyed through a so-called Christian message that is not centered upon Jesus Christ – the Holy One – in the fear of the LORD, is foreign to what is presented in Scripture. It is **"another gospel."** (2 Cor. 11:4; Gal. 1:6-10; Col. 2:8, 18-19) The Bible tells us that **"the fear of the LORD"** is the very **"beginning of wisdom"** and **"the beginning of knowledge."** (Ps. 111:10; Prov. 1:7) We know that the one who fears Him obeys Him and is blessed to be comforted by Him (Ps. 119:165; Prov. 14:26,-27; 22:4; Acts 9:31).

Until one rids his mind of every vestige of this evil notion of an unconditional eternal security, he will not be brought to holiness. Until he is purged **"with the washing of water by the word,"** he will hold a false sense of security and will not deal biblically with the sinful self-life. He will see no need in presenting himself to the LORD daily as a **"living sacrifice, holy, acceptable unto God."** (Lk. 9:23-24; Rom. 12:1; Eph. 5:26) Such is said to be **"your reasonable service."**

Regrettably, the Calvinistic mindset of "once saved always saved" permeates the thinking of millions who claim to be followers of Jesus Christ. But Jesus never taught this doctrine, nor did He hint at such a notion. He said that those who are following Him are denying self and taking up their crosses **"daily."** (Lk. 9:23-24) Christ gave no such promise of an unconditional eternal security. Scripture hints of no such thing. There are always conditions attached to His promises (Isa. 1:18-20; Jn. 10:27-29; 15:1-6; Heb. 3:6, 12-15). The honest observer will notice that eternal security is only promised to those who presently know Him, are hearing His voice, following Him, and abiding in Him.

No single doctrine or inner thought so thoroughly circumvents the daily cross as does this evil, unbiblical lie of "once saved always saved." Such a diabolical falsehood robs from its deceived adherents all fear of God and urgency to obey Christ's command to deny self, take up the cross **"daily,"** and follow Him (Lk. 9:23-24).

The enemy of souls told the very first man that he would still remain in God's grace if he disobeyed the command of his Maker (Gen. 2:17). What happened when the man and woman sinned? (Gen. 3:4) The curse was incurred as they were ushered right out of His fellowship and presence. — **"Therefore the LORD God sent him forth from the garden of Eden ... So he drove out the man ..."** (Gen. 3:23-24)

When one begins to be purged of this serpentine seed, he will cease to hold on to the false and unfounded hope that he is secure while living in sin (Rom. 6:1-2, 15; Gal. 5:19-21; 1 Cor. 6:9-10; Rev. 21:8, 27). The true follower of Christ makes no excuse for sin, but rather readily confesses his sin and repents of it before the God who told us He is **"holy, holy, holy"** and soon returning for His Bride, which is **"a glorious church, not having spot, or wrinkle, or any such thing; but that it should be holy and without blemish."** (Eph. 5:26-27)

> **"...Christ also loved the church, and gave himself for it; (why did Jesus come and die?) That he might sanctify and cleanse it with the washing of water by the word, That he might present it to himself a glorious church, not having spot, or wrinkle, or any such thing; but that it should be holy and without blemish." Ephesians 5:25-27**

The believer, who has been found and saved because of Christ's sacrifice, is in a war for his own soul. According to the One who is our Salvation, in the believer's patience (perseverance) he will possess eternal life in Christ (Lk. 21:19). Anyone want to argue with Jesus?

> "Dearly beloved, I beseech *you* as strangers and pilgrims, abstain from fleshly lusts, which war against the soul." 1 Peter 2:11

The enduring disciple must obey the One who bought him with His blood to remain in His eternal kingdom (Matt. 7:21-29; Lk. 6:26). To **"fight"** and to **"lay hold on eternal life"** are commanded:

> "Fight the good fight of faith, lay hold on eternal life, whereunto thou art also called, and hast professed a good profession before many witnesses. I give thee charge in the sight of God, who quickeneth all things, and *before* Christ Jesus, who before Pontius Pilate witnessed a good confession; That thou keep *this* commandment without spot, unrebukeable, until the appearing of our Lord Jesus Christ." 1 Timothy 6:12-14

In light of His soon return, 2 Peter 3 speaks of the necessity of being found in Christ **"without spot, and blameless."**

> "Wherefore, beloved, seeing that ye look for such things, be diligent that ye may be found of him in peace, without spot, and blameless." 2 Peter 3:14

The true disciple is to ever trust in Jesus, as he is to be of a dependent spirit – one that is **"poor."** For only the **"poor in spirit"** are going to see the LORD in His holy Heaven (Matt. 5:3-8). The Savior warned, **"Blessed *are* the poor in spirit: for theirs is the kingdom of heaven."** (Matt. 5:3) To be **"poor in spirit"** here means to be *broken, destitute, spiritually impoverished*, and *desperate* for the LORD, realizing one's own complete hopelessness in himself and without the grace of Christ (Ps. 39:5; Isa. 64:6). This is what Jesus taught is the heart posture of His true people. The woeful doctrine of **"ease"** is taught by **"ungodly men"** who are **"turning the grace of our God into lasciviousness (no restraint** from sinning; license to sin), and denying the only Lord God, and our Lord Jesus Christ." (Amos 6:1; Jude 3-4) Such a concept is to be contended against vigorously and diligently.

> "Beloved, when I gave all diligence to write unto you of the common salvation, it was needful for me to write unto you, and exhort *you* that ye should earnestly contend for the faith which was once delivered unto the saints. For there are certain men crept in unawares, who were before of old ordained to this condemnation, ungodly men, turning the grace of our God into lasciviousness (license for sin), and denying the only Lord God, and our Lord Jesus Christ." Jude 3-4

Our LORD never taught that after being saved, His people are unconditionally eternally secure. This is the teaching of evil and presumptuous men, who are to be earnestly contended against until they either repent or are driven away. Without exception, such unbiblical mythology causes those who espouse it to be **"at ease in Zion,"** and many of them **"fall away."** (Amos 6:1; Lk. 8:13) **"Woe unto them,"** says the Almighty! They are **"settled on their lees"** and indulging in the **"abundance of idleness."** (Ezek. 16:39; Zeph. 1:12) Being **"at ease in Zion"** or **"lukewarm"** is shown in Scripture to be an accursed posture of heart and way of life, and not true security whatsoever, but rather the symptom of sure damnation (Jer. 48:10-18; Amos 6:1; Zeph. 1:12; Rev. 3:15-16).

> "And it shall come to pass at that time, *that* I will search Jerusalem with candles, and <u>punish the men that are settled on their lees: that say in their heart, The LORD will not do good, neither will he do evil</u>." Zephaniah 1:12

There are multitudes like this today. They must be reached with the message of the cross. I am talking about millions of people who are comfortable in their social club like local churches, believing they are secure for Heaven, and yet they are going to be cast alive for eternity into the bowels of eternal damnation. These people are card-carrying members of their churches and denominations, participants at non-denominational local churches, etc. They have a **"form of godliness"** and yet deny the daily lordship, authority, or **"power"** of Jesus to rule over their personal lives (2 Tim. 3:5).

> **"I know thy works, that thou art neither cold nor hot: I would thou wert cold or hot. So then because thou art lukewarm, and neither cold nor hot, I will spew (vomit) thee out of my mouth." Revelation 3:15-16**

"Lukewarm" means tepid, and refers to an apostate or backslidden spiritual state that is sure to end in eternal damnation if the person refuses to repent and return to the LORD. Who is Jesus addressing here? The Church, not those who were never saved. These people had clearly fallen away due to not remaining true to the One who was previously their **"first love."**

To the Ephesian church, Jesus said:

> **"Nevertheless I have somewhat against thee, because thou hast left thy first love. Remember therefore from whence thou art fallen, and repent, and do the first works; or else I will come unto thee quickly, and will remove thy candlestick out of his place, except thou repent." Revelation 2:4-5**

According to these words from our LORD, repentance is the beginning of God's recovery of His people from the state of losing our **"first love"** – Jesus. As long as He is our **"first**

love," He is first place in our lives, and all else revolves around loving and serving Him. As He is first place, we will keep under our bodies for the joy of knowing Him and escaping the wrath to come. He's coming soon, beloved!

As seen in Revelation 2 and 3, falling away into lukewarmness clearly occurs after one has been saved (1 Cor. 9:27-10:12). In fact, they could not have fallen from grace unless they had first been saved by grace (Gal. 5:4; Heb. 12:15). Their souls were therefore in danger of being rejected – vomited out – by Christ (Lk. 8:13; Jn. 6:66; 1 Tim. 4:1; 2 Pet. 2:20-22; Rev. 2:4-5; 3:15-16).

"Abundance of idleness" was one of the sins of Sodom (Ezek. 16:49). In light of His sudden return, Jesus warned us not to be caught off guard in the state of **"surfeiting,"** which is over eating or over-indulgence in the things of this world (Lk. 21:34-36).

> **"Take heed, brethren, lest there be in any of you an evil heart of unbelief, in departing from the living God. But exhort one another daily, while it is called To day; lest any of you be hardened through the deceitfulness of sin. For we are made partakers of Christ, if we hold the beginning of our confidence stedfast unto the end; While it is said, To day if ye will hear his voice, harden not your hearts, as in the provocation." Hebrews 3:12-15**

Many a Bible truth should be fear-inducing to the point of making us ever concerned that our relationship with Christ is on fire and not lukewarm, at ease, or cold.

The person who is not afraid to backslide, who sees no possible danger in growing cold toward the LORD, is already backslidden!

According to Jesus' last days warning, there is a danger of growing callous and cold toward Christ and His people.

> **"And then shall many be offended, and shall betray one another, and shall hate one another. And many false prophets shall rise, and shall deceive many. And because iniquity shall abound, the love of many shall wax cold. But he that shall endure unto the end, the same shall be saved." Matthew 24:10-13**

Recently, a fellow brother and minister of Christ shared his concern that his love for Christ was waxing cold. This older and genuine man of God is very wise in the LORD and broken. Because of this, he is transparent about his daily and desperate need to be ever drawing nearer to the Savior. For this purpose, he shared his concern and we prayed. I was then privileged to continue to lift up his request for him to again wax hot for Jesus, and to be fully recovered out of coldness.

To be lukewarm toward a God who came in the flesh to die for us **"while we were yet sinners"** and bring us into His eternal family and home, is inexcusable and grave sin (Jn. 14:1-6; Rom. 5:6, 8; 1 Tim. 3:16).

> **"And that he died for all, that they which live should not henceforth live unto themselves, but unto him which died for them, and rose again." 2 Corinthians 5:15**

> **"And from Jesus Christ, who is the faithful witness, and the first begotten of the dead, and the prince of the kings of the earth. Unto him that loved us, and washed us from our sins in his own blood." Revelation 1:5**

To be lukewarm is to have another god in His place, which is idolatry (Exod. 20:3). The LORD told us that He is a jealous God and that He greatly delights in us, His people (Exod. 34:14; Ps. 16:3). Overcoming the soul-damning sin of idolatrous lukewarmness can only come by the intentional, forthright, and deliberate choice to lift up, elevate and put Jesus first place, and to hate this world and the things in it (Jn. 12:32; Eph. 5:5-9; James 4:4-10; 1 Jn. 2:14-17). The apostle Paul said that he kept his flesh crucified – dead to lukewarmness, crass indifference, coldness, this fleeting world, and luxurious and over-indulgent living (Lk. 12:35-40; 21:34-36; 1 Cor. 9:27; Gal. 2:20; 6:14; Rev. 3:15-16).

The Bible speaks to us about being **"fervent in spirit,"** which means maintaining zeal to the boiling point (Rom. 12:11).

If the disciple drifts and becomes lukewarm, and if he doesn't keep himself crucified with Christ, he will then fall into the five sins that kept the covenant people of God out of their Promised Land (1 Cor. 9:27-10:12).

> **"But God forbid that I should glory, save in the cross of our Lord Jesus Christ, by whom the world is crucified unto me, and I unto the world." Galatians 6:14**

Glorying in or taking up the cross which Jesus told us to pick up, will keep crucified the deeds of the body and facilitate a glorious hotness toward Jesus, our **"first love."** (Rev. 2:4-5)

The lukewarm are overtaken with **"the deceitfulness of sin"** and are **"at ease in Zion."** (Amos 6:1; Heb. 3:12-15) They have created a god in their own image that accepts them just as they choose to live. They have not sought to discover what the Judge told us in His Holy Word, and are therefore (in many cases) without that knowledge, and yet will still be judged against that holy Standard (Jn. 12:48; Rom. 2:16; Rev. 20:11-15). Didn't He forewarn us that people would be destroyed **"for lack of knowledge"?** (Hos. 4:6) God **"Hath in these last days spoken unto us by *his* Son, whom he hath appointed heir of all things,"** and therefore all men are **"without excuse."** (Rom. 1:20; Heb. 1:2) Not only do conscience and creation make known His existence and judgment to come, so does His Word (Ps. 19:1; Lk. 16:17, 29-31; Rom. 1:19-20).

Jesus came and gave us His Word, and we are therefore **"without excuse."** (Rom. 1:20)

> **"If I had not come and spoken unto them, they had not had sin: but now they have no cloak for their sin." John 15:22**

The backslidden people today who once served the LORD, erroneously surmise in their hearts that the LORD is not going to reward His people for their heart intentions, motives, actions, or works (1 Pet. 4:17-19). The Word tells us that **"the LORD shall judge his people."** (Heb. 10:30) He says He is going to **"punish"** this evil practice of crafting a god in their own image according to their own evil imagination (Gen. 6:3-5; Jer. 17:9; 2 Cor. 10:3-6). It would be better never to have known Jesus, than after knowing Him, to turn away from Him (2 Pet. 2:20-22).

To those who delight in His law, His **"commandments are not grievous."** (1 Jn. 5:3) They **"delight to do"** His will (Ps. 40:8; 119:35).

Are you beginning to see how important it is to **"keep under"** your body and fleshly desires?

> **"And they that are Christ's have crucified the flesh with the affections and lusts." Galatians 5:24**

In viewing the cross we are commanded to take up, perhaps the key is understanding that God enables all who obey Him. He grants divine mercy, enablement, and power over the flesh to those who come to Him through the Great Intercessor, broken and emptied of self (Heb. 4:14-16; 7:24-26). When we draw near to Him, He draws near to us with His power to break all yokes that bind us to the earthly, and blesses us to function as He has directed. It is then that **"the law of the Spirit of life in Christ Jesus"** makes us **"free from the law of sin and death."** (Rom. 8:1-4; Eph. 3:7; 4:7) Those who love Him seek and obey Him (1 Jn. 2:3-6).

Perhaps Andrew Murray well captured the essence of this truth of the grace and cross of Christ when he wrote these words:

> *"'In him is no sin. Whosoever abideth in him sinneth not.'* When abiding in Christ becomes close and unbroken, so that the soul lives from moment to moment in perfect union with the Lord its keeper, He does, indeed, keep down the power of the old nature, so that it does not regain dominion over the soul ... Ignorance of the promise or unbelief or unwatchfulness opens the door for sin to reign ... *'In him is no sin. Whosoever abideth in him sinneth not.'* Jesus does indeed save him from his sin – not by the removal of his sinful nature, but by keeping him from yielding to it ... The union and fellowship is the secret of a holy life: *'In him is no sin. Whosoever abideth in him sinneth not.'" Abide in Christ,* pp. 213-214

One is not alone in living the victorious life – the Savior is with us **"lo ... always ... even unto the end of the world. Amen."** (Matt. 28:20) After God finds and saves us through the perfect and complete work of Christ, thereby making us His children, He does not abandon us. Yet, He does require our participation.

"Wherefore, my beloved, as ye have always obeyed, not as in my presence only, but now much more in my absence, work out your own salvation with fear and trembling. For it is God which worketh in you both to will and to do of his good pleasure." Philippians 2:12-13

"For if ye live after the flesh, ye shall die: but <u>if ye through the Spirit</u> do mortify the deeds of the body, ye shall live." Romans 8:13

His grace enables the fullness of joy, and the glorious pleasing of Him who is worthy of all our worship (Eph. 3:7; 4:7). His grace is freely given to those who humble themselves before Him. His grace is their fuel, their enablement to please Him. It labors in their hearts and lives (1 Cor. 15:10).

"God is love." 1 John 4:16

The counterfeit looks for a way around the cross instead of through it. Because he refuses to love Christ enough, he is not granted the grace to overcome, and is himself overcome by the evil working within him which Christ would otherwise have subdued. He looks in vain for a way out of the authentic and saving faith, which always produces literal and practical obedience to the Lord (1 Jn. 2:3-6). A faith that doesn't produce fruit and works pleasing to the LORD, is a false faith that will prevent that deceived soul from entering the gates of eternal glory (Matt. 3:7-8, 10; 7:16-21; Tit. 1:16; 1 Jn. 2:3-5; 3:8-10; James 2).

"One thing have I desired of the LORD, that will I seek after; that I may dwell in the house of the LORD all the days of my life, to behold the beauty of the LORD, and to enquire in his temple." Psalms 27:4

The true disciple desires more and more of Christ, and has willingly and obediently laid down his whole being to obtain this **"one thing"** of knowing Him (Jn. 17:3). Not only David but also Paul had this as his all-consuming goal and purpose.

> **"That I may know him, and the power of his resurrection, and the fellowship of his sufferings, being made conformable unto his death."** Philippians 3:10

There is nothing as important to the remnant disciple as that one prize of being with his Savior now and forever. He is willing to endure anything, even martyrdom. Nothing would be too much to pay, to experience communion with Jesus both now and throughout endless ages and beyond. This is the very **"mark"** Paul told us that he pressed toward.

> **"Brethren, I count not myself to have apprehended: but *this* one thing *I do*, forgetting those things which are behind, and reaching forth unto those things which are before, I press toward the mark for the prize of the high calling of God in Christ Jesus."** Philippians 3:13-14

The brazen eternal security proponent, with no Scripture to validate his heresy, forges ahead as he vainly imagines that he has no need to take up his cross and follow Christ. He relishes the victory Jesus wrought on *Calvary's* cross, and yet refuses to take up the cross this same Savior commands and requires *him* to carry (Lk. 9:23-24). The moral coward will have no part in crucifixion of the self-life, so he migrates to the evil and diabolical error of Calvinism.

Paul had no such posture and neither does any true disciple today. All who love Him in truth are sober, fervent, watchful, and prayerful without ceasing as they look for the soon return of their LORD (Lk. 12:35-40; Heb. 9:28).

In stark contrast to those who are arrogantly and ignorantly **"at ease"** in their falsehood of an unconditional eternal security, the apostle Paul says here: **"Brethren, I count NOT myself to have apprehended: but *this* one thing I do..."** This great servant and apostle of Christ did not count himself to have obtained the crown of righteousness just yet. It wasn't until later, just before his decease, that Paul said, **"I have fought a good fight, I have finished *my* course, I have kept the faith: Henceforth there is laid up for me a crown of righteousness, which the Lord, the righteous judge, shall give me at that day: and not to me only, but unto all them also that love his appearing."** (2 Tim. 4:7-8)

> **"Blessed are the poor in spirit (those desperate for Jesus): for theirs is the kingdom of heaven."**
> **Matthew 5:3**

It is clear to see that the apostle Paul was **"poor in spirit."** (Matt. 5:3) He was ever mindful that without Christ's grace and righteousness, he was destitute. This servant and apostle was perpetually desperate for the LORD, and as a spiritual pauper without Him, utterly in need of His holy grace. This is why we see him keeping under his sinful nature and pressing **"toward the mark for the prize of the high calling of God in Christ Jesus,"** which was to **"know him, and the power of his resurrection, and the fellowship of his sufferings, being made conformable unto his death; If by any means I might attain unto the resurrection of the dead."** (1 Cor. 9:27; Phil. 3:10-14)

Did you note here in Philippians 3 that Paul speaks of **"the fellowship of his sufferings, being made conformable unto his death; If by any means I might attain unto the resurrection of the dead"**? In other words, the only hope he had of attaining to the resurrection of the dead with Christ was to truly **"know him"** and to suffer with Him, **"being made conformable unto his death."**

Make no mistake: Any and all leaders who are not preaching this same cross that Jesus and Paul preached – that you must die that Christ might live – are themselves perishing (not saved), and are the very **"ministers"** of Satan (Matt. 16:22-23; 1 Cor. 1:18; 2 Cor. 11:11-15). They are **"enemies of the cross of Christ."** (Gal. 1:6-10; Phil. 3:17-19) Those who do not regularly preach the propitiatory cross of Christ, and the cross He commanded for all who will follow Him to take up, are preaching another gospel and are therefore **"accursed."** (Gal. 1:6-9)

Those who do not obey the biblical message of the cross can never experience truly knowing Him and His resurrection power (Phil. 3:10).

Concerning the crucified life, Bill Wegener writes:

> "There is a beauty in understanding this. When we understand the true nature of what the law reveals us to be and what happened on the cross, we then and only then understand the depravity of our own souls and realize what a great price He paid and that everything else is foolishness. The closer I get to the Lord, the more I realize what a wretched person I am. The beauty is that it's this understanding that brings the true joy of salvation in Jesus Christ. We no longer have to strive with futility for the worldly desires that are never ever fulfilled."

Satan is the champion of self-love and is the god of those in leadership who teach it (Isa. 14:12-15). He is lord of all who do not continually preach the cross of Christ (2 Tim. 3:1-7). Scripture says their **"god is their belly,"** referring to the fact that such teachers worship the god of their own self-serving agenda because their lives are not laid down and submitted to Jesus (Gal. 5:24; Phil. 3:17-19). The last days promise to see an epidemic rise in such self-love and beguilers who teach others to love self instead of denying self (Lk. 9:23-24; 2 Tim. 3:1-13).

When one is truly **"poor in spirit,"** he realizes, like Paul, that he is **"desperately wicked"** without the present grace of God, and that he must **"die daily"** to remain in his place with the LORD, lest he **"fail of the grace of God."** (Jer. 17:9; Rom. 7:18, 24; Heb. 12:15) According to the Holy Scriptures, failing the grace of God *is* possible. If failing divine grace were not possible, such words as we find in Hebrews 12 would not be in the Bible:

> **"Follow peace with all** *men,* **and holiness, without which no man shall see the Lord: Looking diligently lest any man fail of the grace of God; lest any root of bitterness springing up trouble** *you,* **and thereby many be defiled." Hebrews 12:14-15**

Re-read this passage and note closely here, as is evident throughout Holy Writ, the urgency toward and necessity of personal holiness.

PRAYER: *Father in Heaven, thank You for sending Your only begotten Son for the sins of the whole world. Right this moment and afresh, I lay my life in Thine holy hands and release my whole being to You. I love You, Jesus, and thank You for multiplying Your holy grace to me this moment, and filling me afresh with Your Holy Ghost. Let there be fruit, more fruit, and much fruit born through our relationship communion. Amen.*

Capture Points

1. Discuss 1 Corinthians 9:27.

2. On an index card, write out Romans 8:29 (KJV recommended).

3. Transcribe Galatians 5:24 and 6:14 on an index card (KJV recommended).

4. Discuss and mediate upon Philippians 3:10.

ADDENDUM

MAKING PEACE WITH GOD

Entering the Kingdom

"But your iniquities (sins) have separated between you and your God, and your sins have hid his face from you, that he will not hear." Isaiah 59:2

God is holy and our sins separate us from Him. We have all broken God's laws by lying, dishonoring our parents, cheating, hating, committing a sex act in our mind with someone we are not married to, stealing, coveting, taking His holy name in vain, etc. These are all sins against God and we are all guilty. *Committing any single one of these sins makes us guilty of breaking the whole law and worthy of death.*

Divine justice demands that our violations be punished. Because we are guilty of breaking God's holy law, we deserve to be fairly repaid for our offenses. God doesn't want us to be punished in hell forever though, so He sent His Son to pay the debt for us, so we would not have to pay for our own sins in eternal hell as we clearly deserve, but rather live now and forever with Him. What love!

At the end of a perfect (sinless) life, Christ carried the very cross He was to be nailed to. His infinite love for you, along with the nails driven through His hands and feet, held Him to that cross as He agonized for 6 hours in pain - to pay for your sins. He was crucified to make peace between God and man. The Son of God bridged the gap that sin had caused. This wonderful man named Jesus chose to shed His life blood (die - in excruciating pain) for you rather than live without you. He loves you.

> **"For the wages of sin is death; but the gift of God is eternal life through Jesus Christ our Lord." Romans 6:23**

Christ died to fully pay for the sins of the human race (John 19:30). God loves all men and wants us to experience relationship with Him, now and forever (John 17:3). Friend, who else has ever died for you but Jesus, the Good Shepherd?

> **"For when we were yet without strength, in due time Christ died for the ungodly (that's you)." Romans 5:6**

> **"Christ Jesus came into the world to save (rescue) sinners." 1 Timothy 1:15**

No religion or religious figure can save your soul from hell (no matter what they claim). Jesus didn't come to start a religion but rather to establish His eternal kingdom in the hearts of men, granting them a relationship with God. Jesus Christ is the only One who bears nail-scarred hands and feet for your sins. He is the *only* way to God and your only hope.

> **"For there is ONE God, and ONE mediator between God and men, the man Christ Jesus." 1 Timothy 2:5**

The Son of God died and rose again to take away all your sins. He was the only One qualified for the job and He is the only One worthy of your worship. Peace with God happens when we meet the Prince of Peace.

Now apply His holy blood to your life so that you may live now and eternally with Him. You must completely turn your life over to Him and turn away from all your sins - repent. Now, pray this prayer to God with all that is within you, from your heart and out loud: "Dear Lord Jesus, thank You for shedding Your holy blood for my sins to save me from eternal damnation in hell. You are my only hope. Heavenly Father, I acknowledge all my sins against You right now, and ask Your forgiveness through the precious blood of Jesus, who died and rose again for me. Lord Jesus, take over my life right now and forevermore. I love You. Amen."

Tell another Christian. Find a group of Christ-centered believers who love God's Word. Be water baptized. Read your King James Bible daily and talk with God in prayer. Follow Christ to the end of your life. Sign up for the free email devotionals at SafeGuardYourSoul.com.

GOSPEL TRACTS Available
at SafeGuardYourSoul.com

LOSER

Jesus told us all that only the losers will gain eternal life (Matt. 10:38-39). With the holy law to convict of sin, the necessity of "repentance toward God and faith toward our Lord Jesus Christ," and the holiness of our Maker emphasized, this Gospel tract has already blessed tens of thousands of souls with the knowledge of God. It's very well received among people. The ease of handing this one out is second to none. May God bless the conversations we are able to engage in when handing this one out to the lost and when supplying other Christians.

Read and Order Your Supply Today at SafeGuardYourSoul.com

Diary of a Dead Man

With the horrible cover image, this tract instantly grabs attention of the recipient. While handing it out, one may choose to ask "That's a horrible image, huh?" The person receiving the tract will then say, "Yes, it sure is." To this the believer can respond with, "Please don't end up like that guy." This is also a very easy Gospel tract to distribute with wide appeal and virtually flawless response and receptivity – sure to make your seed sowing journey very fruitful.

Read and Order Your Supply Today at SafeGuardYourSoul. com

JESUS: *Why Did This Man Die On A Cross?*

With millions in print, the JESUS Tract is reaching thousands of lost souls globally and is perhaps the most condensed and complete presentation of the holy law and Gospel available in tract form today. This tract contains a glorious exaltation of the **"Great Shepherd of the sheep,"** *the* **"Good Shepherd"** *who came to pay the complete price for the sins of His fallen creation (Heb. 13:20; Jn. 10:1-10). Order your supply today and begin using these messengers to reach those for whom He died and rose again.*

Read and Order Your Supply Today at SafeGuardYourSoul.com

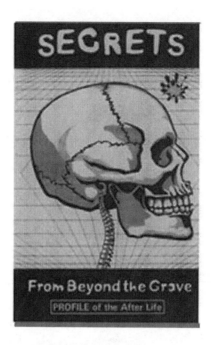

SECRETS *From Beyond the Grave*

Shocking & thought-provoking secrets about the after life. Contains a blistering menu of what awaits all who are not born again. This message is not for those who wish to hide the whole truth about eternal things. SECRETS is a tract few can resist reading with its aesthetic wickedness which reeks of death, and curiosity provoking title.

Read and Order Your Supply Today at SafeGuardYourSoul.com

What People are Saying about the SafeGuard Your Soul Gospel Tracts:

"I walk a wooden cross through the 'Deep Ellum' area of Dallas, so, I get handed a lot of Bible Flyers and tracts. Your *JESUS: Why Did This Man Die On A Cross?* is about the best so far." Jim B., TX

"I've had the hugest response I have ever seen through a tract." Michael, Oregon

"Since 1999 my wife and I began distributing thousands of the *JESUS* tracts in Haiti, Trinidad & Tobago, Ghana, Holland, Nigeria, Vatican City, Italy, France, Japan, Germany, Thailand, Aruba, Cayman Islands, Puerto Rico, and all across America. The *JESUS* tract is quite unique as it presents the gospel clearly and in the power of the Holy Spirit. The Holy Trinity has enabled the publishing of this magnificent gospel tract titled--*JESUS*, that is literally reaching the world. Many of our friends and family members have also used this tract to the glory of God. *We have personally witnessed many souls being won to Christ as a direct result of the JESUS tract.*" Jay, Texas

"I gave out 500 or so of the tracts and the response WAS huge! I will never use another tract than the *JESUS* tract! I have seen DOZENS of people get saved from it!" Aaron, Oregon

"We have read over your tract called, *JESUS-Why did this man die on a cross?* and are in love with it!" Joey Q., Abilene, TX

"We went out passing the *JESUS* tracts. They are so effective. They look so good when you hand them to the people and they see the Name of Jesus there staring at them. We passed so many out today I lost count but I need to order some more of them." Cindy H., Texas

"Thanks so much for the *Secrets From Beyond the Grave...* that tract is so awesome! I can't wait to order them for our halloween outreach this year!" Jeff F.

"Hi Todd! I have been passing out your *JESUS* tracts. I like them...Everyone really likes them, including my son's teenage friends...God bless you Todd!" Chris A., WI

"I love your new tract (**HELL: Don't Go There!**)...Saw two guy's publicly give their trust to Jesus Christ...Thanks for such a wonderful tract Todd. I love you brother." Byron C., TX

"Your tracts have helped me win dozens of souls to Jesus." Jay B., TX

"Your tracts planted the seed that led me to Christ. I was saved after seeing tons of tracts laying all over Wal-Mart while working, shopping, etc." unknown

SHARPENING YOUR
PERSONAL DISCERNMENT

For the Building Up of His Saints

To begin receiving the *Moments for My Master* email
devotionals, sign up at SafeGuardYourSoul.com.
Also, sign up for print newsletter on site.

ANOTHER BOOK

BY TODD TOMASELLA

Raised Up

This volume centers upon the essential cross and resurrection power of the Most High, raising upward the bowed down disciple who waits upon Him in fervent expectancy of His divine life and soon return.

The call of God upon every believer is to die downward that He might raise them upward to fruitfulness in His life and power.

"And the remnant that is escaped of the house of Judah shall again take root downward, and bear fruit upward." Isaiah 37:31

Upward fruit bearing occurs as the disciple takes root downward, being buried down deeply into the death and burial of Christ. The One who is **"the resurrection, and the life"** then simultaneously raises up that downward dying saint to newness of life in His Spirit (Jn. 11:25; Rom. 8:11).

Here is some of what you will learn in the pages of this volume:

- *How to sink down deep into the death and burial of Christ, that God might raise you upward to bear abundant fruit for His glory*

- *The importance of loving and honoring the LORD above self, and seeing His grace and power work in you in ministry to others*

- *How to discern which leaders are teaching the truth from the many wolves among us*

- *How to incorporate the cross in your personal life daily, and live a life fully pleasing to God*

- *The importance of prayer as you expectantly look for the soon and glorious return of the LORD Jesus Christ*

In this poignant and timely volume, the person who is possessed by a self-serving "What's in it for ME" mentality instead of "How can I most please my LORD Jesus," is going to discover just how Luciferic his current views are. It is hoped that he will then be brought to repentance and a laying down of his life, that Christ alone might reign (Isa. 14:12-15; James 4:6-10). Ready or not – Jesus is coming (Lk. 21:34-36). Are you ready?

ANOTHER BOOK

BY TODD TOMASELLA

Deceivers

&

False Prophets

Among Us

THE BOOK SOME LEADERS HOPE YOU NEVER FIND OUT ABOUT

Are there false, fruitless and even deceptive predators in the pulpits of the modern church? If so, are these deceivers leading multitudes to the worship of false gods through their damnable heresies? Are "seeker-friendly" churches creating a new class of "Christians" who have no concept of authentic, Biblical Christianity? Are there leaders who are building their own kingdoms in lieu of God's and doing so on your dime? Are we hearing the full-counsel of the LORD from those in leadership, or the psychology and programs of mere men? Are beguiling emissaries in our midst drawing believers away from pure devotion and intimacy with Jesus Christ? Do these things exist within your local fellowship? Are you truly being instructed in the right ways of the LORD? Explore the answers to these and many more questions in this bold, insightful, and resourceful look at the church world today.

WHAT YOU WILL GAIN FROM READING THIS BOOK:

o   What specific erroneous teachings are circulating in the church world and how to identify and expose them

o   How to discern the genuine leaders who truly follow the Word and Spirit of God, from the false and fruitless who are using God's money to build their own kingdoms

o   How to please the LORD by positioning and establishing His written revelation as final authority in your personal life

o   How to discern and cease wasting your brief existence on this earth supporting wolves in sheep's clothing

o   How to serve God with a loving and concerned heart from the foundation of divine immutable truth

278 Pages

Find out More about this book at www.SafeGuardYourSoul. com

Order this book at www.SafeGuardYourSoul.com

For the latest resources, please visit www. SafeGuardYourSoul.com

ANOTHER BOOK

BY TODD TOMASELLA

LIE of the Ages

History's Fatal Falsehood

Lie of the Ages is a sound and extensive biblical annihilation of the first lie told to mankind - a falsehood that has rung through the corridors of history. This book is a thorough expose' of why this dangerous heresy, still widely taught today, is so destructive to the souls of men and the true Church of Jesus Christ.

740 Pages

Contains more than 57 life-changing prayers.

Find out more about this book at www.SafeGuardYourSoul.com

About the Author

Todd Tomasella is in utter and perpetual need of divine grace on a momentary basis. God be praised for His gracious loving kindness through our LORD Jesus Christ and the infinite supply of His love towards us whom He has apprehended for His purposes (Ps. 138:8; Phil. 1:6; 2:12-13; 1 Jn. 3:1).

May the LORD do His ever-deepening work in each of us, perfecting that which concerns us, as He, our Potter, molds us – His clay – into His holy image (Jer. 18:1-6; Rom. 8:29).

Todd Tomasella is a publisher of Gospel literature designed to strike the lost with the fear of God and to build up the body of Christ. Based in Dallas, Texas, Todd is blessed to possess divine grace with a kingdom perspective as he serves through discipleship-pastoring and evangelism on a daily basis and in a local fellowship, Scripture-intensive books, Gospel tracts, the website SafeGuardYourSoul.com, the *Moments for My Master* email devotionals, and speaking engagements.

Without Christ, Todd can do **"nothing."** (Jn. 15:5)

Visit www.SafeGuardYourSoul.com

Made in the USA
Middletown, DE
22 August 2018